THE COURAGE
OF HIS CONVICTIONS

The Courage

'I'll willingly gamble away a third of my life
in prison, so long as I can live the way I want
for the other two-thirds.'

TONY PARKER &
ROBERT ALLERTON

Of His Convictions

HUTCHINSON OF LONDON

HUTCHINSON & CO. (*Publishers*) LTD
178–202 Great Portland Street, London, W.1

London Melbourne Sydney
Auckland Bombay Toronto
Johannesburg New York

First published March 1962
Second impression March 1962

*This book has been set in Baskerville type face. It has
been printed in Great Britain by The Anchor Press,
Ltd., in Tiptree, Essex, on Antique Wove paper and
bound by Taylor Garnett Evans & Co., Ltd., in
Watford, Herts*

For
PAUL STEPHENSON
without whom it would not have been written

The proper examination of recidivist cases is only in its infancy. . . . Such systematic work as has been done on unselected groups indicates that a very considerable number of them suffer either from pathological stigmata or have acquired these stigmata through penological mishandling. Until proper measures of investigation have been applied it is really absurd to draw hard and fast conclusions on the subject.

EDWARD GLOVER: *The Concept of Recidivism*, 1955
(*By kind permission of Edward Glover and the publishers, the Imago Publishing Co.*)

While the precise aetiology of delinquency and crime must vary with each individual case, the broad conditions which generate and stimulate them are well known. It is the final eradication of such conditions which can alone provide the only sure guarantee against the continued presence of anti-social behaviour which involves the community in expense which is not limited to the financial sphere.

TERENCE MORRIS: *The Criminal Area*, 1958
(*By kind permission of Terence Morris and the publishers, Routledge & Kegan Paul.*)

Contents

Introduction

I FIRST met Robert Allerton in prison, where he was captive and I was not. The only thing we appeared to have in common was our age, both of us being in our early thirties.

He was a powerful broad-shouldered Cockney: he had been educated in the streets of the East End and approved school, and had spent his childhood in poverty and much of his manhood in prison; and he had a long record of violent crime. I was a small Mancunian from a middle-class background, with a steady job and a wife and three children.

We were both nervous, and conversation was not easy. Knowing he had a record of violence, I expected some show of toughness: there was none. As I had neither authority nor power over him, there was no reason I could think of for his being apprehensive. But he plainly was, and continued to be for a long time. It was only gradually that I came to understand why.

In prison there are no half-measures: one is either in or out. There are only two categories—prisoners and 'Them'. The second includes not only the Governor and staff, but all others —doctors, chaplains, social workers, instructors, clerks, visitors, teachers—who do not wear the prison blue. The gulf between is wide and deep. Anyone who tries to cross it from the prisoners' side, by becoming a Redband or trusted prisoner for instance, is regarded as a weakling and a sycophant. In a recidivist prison like the one Bob was in, they usually are.

And within the 'in' group of prisoners there is another smaller and exclusive one, a Cliveden Set of hard cases who keep away from 'Them' and also sharply separate themselves from the other inmates. They consider themselves the élite.

Acceptance into this group is not earned easily, and depends not only on a man's behaviour inside prison but on his reputation out of it—which is not judged on his own assessment. If he tries too hard to establish himself as tough by describing the violence he has used in committing crime or avoiding arrest, he will be avoided because he talks too much, even if most of what he says is true. Nor does violence itself necessarily bring respect: if he has used it too often, or with too slight provocation, he will be considered a nut-case who brings trouble to his associates. A professional criminal looks upon himself as someone who uses violence only when necessary, not for self-indulgence. The other criterion—behaviour inside prison—is measured by how a man currently behaves and, more importantly, how he behaved during previous sentences. If he has been known to take any step towards the side of authority, however small, he will be 'unreliable'. And to be this means complete proscription.

Bob belonged to this clique, and had always done since he first went into prison. Association with me was not only a betrayal of principle, but threatened his social standing and would bring immediate rejection if it was known. Yet it might in fact have been this which made him determined to continue the acquaintance, at least until he could decide for himself whether it was worth while. As his life story shows, pressure from one direction provokes reaction towards another, and the stronger it is the more obstinate he becomes. But whatever the reason he continued to see me. I think if the situation had been reversed, and I had been the one trying to turn away from my own group, I should have given up, because the effort must have been great and there was no prospect of reward. There were three striking things about him. One was his fundamental lack of desire to go straight, another his refusal to attribute his criminality to outside causes, and the third his critical awareness of his own character. They added up to something I was reluctant to acknowledge because it sounded paradoxical—a well-integrated criminal personality.

Gradually he began to express himself more freely. His views were unfailingly contemptuous of everything and everybody. The Prime Minister, Terence Rattigan, Sir Stanley Unwin, even Manchester United—they were all found wanting and tossed aside. Between, he told stories about himself designed to illustrate serious moral deficiencies, ranging wider and more wildly all the time. In return I presented an assiduously cultivated non-committal attitude which can only have seemed disagreeably condescending.

Then fortunately one evening the barriers collapsed. We were talking about poncing, and he said he thought it was disgusting and reprehensible. I replied stiffly that it might be looked upon in some ways as a form of social service, whereupon he launched into a violent attack on the hypocrisy of this studied liberalism with all the fervour of a fundamentalist. The resulting poses of outraged morality were so unfitting to both of us that we laughed—and after that it was no longer necessary ever again for him to attempt to shock, or for me to be so determinedly detached. We relaxed, were able to be ourselves, and began gradually to discover an empathy which has remained and grown.

It was clearly understood by both of us when he came out of prison that there was no question of his going straight. He brusquely refused my tentative offer to help him find a job, and would not even let me meet him at the gate on the morning of his release. He explained politely that this would embarrass him because some of his friends would be there. We made an imprecise arrangement to meet a few days afterwards, which did not mature. I didn't expect to see him again.

But a few weeks later we walked into each other in the street; we made another arrangement for a meeting, and this time it succeeded. We have met many times since and have now after two years formed a friendship which will continue, I think, whatever direction either of us takes in the future.

In all that time he has consistently refused to accept anything from me in the way of help or assistance of any kind, even when he has needed it. Yet this, after all, is only a superficial mark of integrity, and much more important are his honesty and directness, his frankness and lack of pretence. In these respects he is outstanding among people I know, and friendship with him has been a rich and enlightening experience.

He has taught me a great deal—and most clearly of all that 'a criminal' is neither a type nor even a category. He has peculiarities, but he is not peculiar. To meet, talk to, and be with him is the same as doing these things with any other man, except possibly that Bob is more straightforward about himself than many. His lack of ambition to reform, at first puzzling, now seems natural; his rejection of the idea for himself no more surprising than a surgeon's if someone suggested he should take up the fish-and-chip trade. He does not even pause to reflect. Some months ago he had the opportunity of learning a business and being paid while he did it: his refusal was immediate and automatic. He thinks of himself as a criminal by vocation, as others follow a calling for teaching or go on the stage.

His moral principles are high. He admires Danilo Dolci and Albert Schweitzer. He opposes the H-bomb, apartheid, anti-semitism and capital punishment. There is nothing insincere about these attitudes—other men, better and worse than him, hold them genuinely too. And perhaps it is no more surprising to find a criminal against hanging on moral grounds than it is to find a bishop condoning it on Christian ones.

This code of values is of course not flawless, and to attack and point out inconsistencies is easy. But the only acknowledgement will be a shrug. He has reached his views after thought and experience like anyone else; and they satisfy him.

Meeting him, it is necessary to remind oneself constantly that he has done, and will still do, acts of violence which are primitive and inexcusable, that there are aspects of his character as dark as the far side of the moon. He has been described at different times by upholders of law and order as 'a hooligan', 'a thug', and 'a man devoid of all decency'. He is all these—at some times, and in some ways. But he is also sensitive, generous, humane. The condemnations no more sum up his whole nature than the praise. Like any other man he is a diamond of different facets which, as it is turned, alternately catch the light. Which do, depend much upon the observer's point of view and even more on the diamond's movements.

It might be tempting to dismiss him into some easily assumed psychiatric category such as 'psychopath'. But to do this, accurately or not, contributes nothing and discards too lightly the positive characteristics. His achievements in widening his own knowledge, in sustaining his mental capacities through frequent imprisonments; his searching for other values; his avoidance of self-pity; even some aspects of his aggressive individualism—these are all worth emphasizing because they contradict the idea of his being irredeemable.

How the vitality of his spirit could find expression in society instead of against it, how it could be harnessed into less socially objectionable channels, is not something which I am qualified or able to answer. I still hope, perhaps unreasonably, for better things—not from him but for him: for escape from the pitiful certainty of crime, conviction, and imprisonment.

Next time the punishment will be severe. At his age and

with his record he will be liable for preventive detention, a sentence of anything between five and fourteen years. By current fashion it will probably be seven or eight—and will turn him, as it has turned most others who have received it, from a young man into an old and senseless one. Prisoners themselves have an expressive phrase: 'He's done so much bird he's twittering.'

The problem he presents, that of the unreformed and unrepentant criminal who is so much at odds with society that he has formed a viable asocial pattern of his own, is one scarcely yet touched.

In the past six months we have talked, often late into the night, with a tape-recorder. This book has been made from the recordings. All the vocabulary, descriptions, and ideas are Robert Allerton's; my part has been mainly to prompt him, arrange and edit the material, and try to show him as the man he is. I have not succeeded: his personality is warmer and more appealing than print can reveal. There is no way I can convey the self-deprecatory shrugs with which he avoids being pompous, the tentativeness of his conclusions, his self-mocking smile. He says many things here which seem brash, and the fault is mine for omitting, because they read tediously, innumerable 'maybes' and 'I'm only guessing buts . . .'

Thanks are especially due to Paul Stephenson, B.B.C. Talks Producer, who first gave Robert Allerton the opportunity to express himself in a short broadcast; to Graham Nicol of Hutchinson's who heard it, and suggested both the book and its title; to Jean Worswick who typed the manuscript; and to my wife Margery for her continual interest, help, and encouragement.

TONY PARKER
Brentwood, Essex

The Record

NAME	*Robert Henry Allerton*
AGE	*33*
CONVICTIONS	*9*
TOTAL SENTENCES	*18 years*
TIME SPENT IN PRISON	*12½ years*
OFFENCES	*Theft*
	Housebreaking
	Warehouse breaking
	Safe blowing
	Smash-and-grab
	Armed robbery
	Assault on police
	Robbery with violence
	Carrying firearms
	Grievous bodily harm

'I don't say I've never had a chance, because I have, I've had plenty of chances. . . .'

'I've no intention of going straight, I'm just being more careful, that's all. . . .'

I

The Thread of Violence

I

The Child Becomes an Outlaw

THE FUNNY thing is, my father was straight. Sometimes I
think if he hadn't been I mightn't have taken to crime. But
I'm only guessing. Probably it wouldn't have made any
difference at all.

My grandfather was a pickpocket, my six uncles were all
villains and tearaways, my brothers and friends were thieves,
and most of the neighbours were in and out of prison like
pigeons in a loft. So for a long time, in fact, my father was the
only straight man I knew.

He was good and kind and honest—but, as I saw it as a kid,
all it got him was poverty. He was a socialist—almost a com-
munist—and he was always talking about changing the system
which brought richness to some and poverty to many. He
believed it could be done by education and political activity, by
arguing and getting people round to his point of view. I was
too impatient for that. I believed the system was wrong, too,
but I knew it wouldn't ever be changed by our sort. I didn't
want to wait two hundred years for the day when everyone had
fair shares. I wanted to take part in the levelling-up of wealth
myself, and make sure *I* got some benefit from it. And I wanted
to start getting on with it there and then.

We lived, the six—then the seven, then the eight—of us, in

two rooms on the top floor of an old terraced house in a side street in Shoreditch. There must have been a time once when the terrace was a posh one in a quiet residential area, but by my day it'd come down a lot. The front elevation looked all right, but the rooms behind were bug-infested and dilapidated, with plaster coming away in lumps, paint peeling off the ceilings, and floorboards and door-jambs split and warped.

The dirtiness of the place worried my mother. She was for ever sweeping and cleaning, trying to get rid of the dust that blew in through the cracks or just seeped from the walls with the constant racket of people moving about. When you live in two rooms for six or eight people you don't have a bedroom and a living-room or fancy divisions like that. There are two rooms with beds and chairs in them, and everything takes place together, most of it at the same time. There were people arguing, fighting, reading, eating, sleeping; and always my mother sweeping, trying to brush clean the spaces in between. She must have taken part in some of the other activities too, but I don't remember it, only her endless swishing about with a brush.

That, and the talk between her and my father. Sometimes in a low tone, murmuring; sometimes angry and desperate and loud. But always about the same thing: the difficulty of finding work.

'Joe's told me there's jobs going down at the docks; I'll try tomorrow.'

'Alice said her old man was working on that demolition for McAdam's at Liverpool Street; why don't you try them?'

'They said at the Labour this won't last long, there's going to be plenty of jobs in the spring.'

I never knew for a long time what my father really did. When I asked my mother, she said proudly: 'He's a top man, and don't you forget it.'

It didn't mean he read *The Times*. When derelict buildings

were being knocked down he was one of those on the roof doing the dangerous work up there—cutting the ground from under his own feet, you might say. Whatever it was, in those days there didn't seem to be much call for it, because he never had regular work. No job lasted more than a week or two, and then he'd be back on the same old tramping around again.

It happened so regularly, so automatically, that I grew up thinking this was what all grown-up work was like—a week or two in, then several weeks out. We always knew which it was by his manner. Friendly and cheerful, skylarking about—he was working. Morose and depressed—he was looking again. Either way he never earned much money, so it didn't make a lot of difference, we were still always poor. My mother never experienced any other way of living than counting pennies and trying to last out till the end of the week. Dinner was usually potatoes or boiled rice, in the evening bread-and-dripping or sometimes stew. But all day long in between there was tea.

I'm not asking for pity on this, though, because it wouldn't be true to say I was unhappy as a kid, or even that poverty meant anything when I was small. Everyone else was in the same boat, and when you grow up with something you accept it because you think it's all there is. There was nothing else to compare it with either, and I didn't have time for comparisons even if there had been. Most of my time was spent outside the house, anyway, and home was only a place to go to for meals and sleep.

Compared with others I've read about, like Gwen Raverat's *Period Piece*, for instance, or Siegfried Sassoon's *Memoirs of a Foxhunting Man*, there was nothing about my childhood particularly fascinating or edifying. But, then, those people had everything laid on and all they had to do was to be sensitive about it. I suppose the same sort of experiences shaped us fundamentally, but in my case life was more concerned with essentials like plain struggle for survival on a material level. I

23

think it was more real, and certainly it was more common, than the life they had. There were no nannies, or horses to ride, but how many people could lead lives like that? There were thousands who had just what I had, to form them into what the upper classes blame them for becoming. Nothing but poverty. That was my childhood, that was the backcloth to it. But the stage-set itself was the street.

Like I said, it was a side one with high terraces that had once looked better. All the windows at ground level, and a lot of those higher up too, were fastened up with strips of paper over the cracks, or boarded over completely where the glass had entirely gone. Once they were broken they stayed like that: repairing them was useless, they only got smashed again by kids throwing things. The front doors were always open, because they weren't anybody's front door, of course, just entrances to places where five or six different families lived. Their frames were warped, anyway, so they couldn't have shut if anyone had wanted them to.

People didn't have dividing lines between their property, at least not for kids. We ran in and out all day long, up and down the stairs, over the walls between the back yards, through the windows, down the shed roofs—you never knew whose house you were in or whose you were coming out of, and nobody bothered about it or even noticed you'd been there.

The street had a market at the top and a Mission Hall near the bottom, an old church in the middle, and a cross-roads with a pub on one corner and a shop that sold everything on the other. There were people moving about all day long, women pushing pram-loads of washing to the baths, out-of-work men loafing, kids chasing one another, fighting, playing, having races with wooden boxes on old pram-wheels.

There wasn't much traffic, but because it was a sort of artery that led to the market there were always costermongers going along with horses and carts, or men pushing barrows. They never bothered about things dropping off, so there was always a litter of cabbage leaves, fruit, bits of wood, old rags, cardboard boxes or occasionally a wooden one. This was an inexhaustible fund of material for kids to play with, and every morning there was the excitement of going out to see what you could find lying about. Everything had value and was put to some kind of use. You ate what was eatable and a few things that were not, and the rest was used for building up barricades, hitting people with, or just slinging about. As the day went on, there was defence of possessions or, much more enjoyable, marauding and looting; and finally the ordinary commerce of barter and exchange.

All the time something was happening, something was going on: there was movement, noise, activity, a great pulse everyone was part of in the bloodstream of the street. There were no colours, only various shades of grey, but it had its own real vitality and life. A painter called L. S. Lowry has got this same thing in his pictures of northern industrial towns: the sense of movement, the business of existence in what first looks like a drab scene. I've never been to the places he paints, but I can see it, and know he's seeing the same thing as I am, and what he's pictured is true.

When it came to Saturday night then the street really took off. Even the bugs in the houses were jumping with excitement. The flares on the stalls up in the market were lit, and everyone seemed to be up there. The pub was full with people drinking as much as they could afford or get tick for, the young men walked around whistling at the girls, those who were too old for it just stood and watched, and the kids tore up and down with less restriction than ever.

In the market itself the stallholders tried to outshout one

25

another for customers, and the narrow lanes between the stalls were jammed with a slowly moving procession, most of whom were just there to look but not to buy. The kids wriggled in and out like fishes, pinching to their hearts' content because everyone was too busy to notice. Sweets, fruit, eggs, winkles, buns—whatever you had a fancy for you could take. Now and then one of the stallholders would catch hold of a couple of kids and give them a halfpenny each to have a fight. Everybody would laugh and egg them on as they flailed away, until one knocked the other into one of the stalls and the man behind it got angry and told them to bugger off out of it.

Bedtime was ten or eleven or twelve o'clock, whatever time you were tired, or got caught by your parents and taken home. Everyone you knew—all your friends and your family, and their friends—were always in the market on a Saturday night, along with all the famous people of the street.

And they were famous too, to us kids. They were the ones who were part of the daily scenery of our lives and seemed to have been there for ever—the tallyman, the bookmaker, the knife-sharpener, the undertaker, the money-lender, the one-man band, the negro who played the spoons, the man with the close-cropped white beard who had a short stick and a red handkerchief at the end of it which he whirled round and round in a fascinating performance that went on for hours. I could never work out how he did it, because the handkerchief wasn't tied to the stick. He could throw it up and catch it folded with the stick inside, then keep it up in the air while he prodded it into a neat square, or made it take on shapes of animals and birds that seemed to balance on the stick. I suppose he was doing it for money originally, but in time he forgot about that side of it and just went on for the sheer enjoyment of his own dexterity, seeing how long he could keep the handkerchief airborne.

The one-man band went around on a bicycle painted in

rainbow colours, with an old clockwork gramophone lashed on the back. He played it when he wanted a rest, but a scratched record was nothing to the noise he could create. He had cymbals on his back, which he worked with his shoulder-blades, and on his chest an arrangement of stiff wire that held up a flute, a trumpet, and a bazooka in front of his mouth. He kept a miniature mouth-organ in his cheek, with his hands he played a banjo, and he worked a drum with his foot. When he was going full blast the noise was incredible, and there was always a crowd round him in the market on Saturday night. Why then especially I don't know, because he was doing exactly the same thing in the street during the week. But somehow he seemed to get inspired on Saturday nights.

I don't know why the tallyman was there then either: it wasn't for business. He must have felt like the rest of us that it was the only place to be, and he wandered around with his pinched face and his tattered raincoat and trilby, and a per-manent drop hanging on the end of his nose. At heart he must have been a kind man, because business was never good and everyone was always behind with their payments, but he never got nasty about it and tried to scare anyone into paying up. He was one of us. That was why he was in the market Saturday nights.

Of all the characters in the street, there was one head and shoulders above the others, in appearance at least—an elderly and very distinguished-looking gentleman with a withered arm. He was always impeccably dressed: his suit had matching jacket and trousers for a start, which was a great rarity, and he wore a silk cravat with a diamond stick-pin. Fake diamond, more than likely, but apart from in the papers nobody'd ever seen a stick-pin. He had gloves, a cane, grey spats, a homburg

hat, and gentleman's boots. Not navvy's boots, you understand, but gentleman's—soft, polished, and neatly laced.

When he walked down the street, nodding gravely to
people he knew, he created a terrific impression of dignity and
refinement. For a long time I thought he was someone special,
a business man from the City perhaps. He called in quite often
at our home, which gave me big standing with the other kids.
I never knew what he came for, because it was always clear he
thought me a nuisance if I hung around. He would come in,
removing his hat and peeling off his gloves and laying them
neatly on the table with his cane. Then he would look at me
sternly and say: 'Off you go now, boy, I want to talk with
your mother.' Or sometimes it would be: 'Here, boy, run up
to the Devonshire and fetch me a bottle of beer.' My mother
would hand me the money and off I went, straight there and
back, not daring to dawdle. He would take it from me with a
nod when I returned, and then jerk his head for me to get
out.

One day he gave me instructions to get him beer when my
mother had no money. Neither had he, so my mother said:
'It'll be all right, Bob, tell them who it's for.' I looked at her
blankly.

'Go on, boy,' he said crossly, 'don't hang about. Go and
get it, and tell them it's for your grandpa.'

That was how I first learned who he was. The man in the
bottle-and-jug at the Devonshire pulled a face when I said the
message, but all the same he gave me the beer.

Even though I was scared of him, I liked him, and he
seemed to like me despite his gruff manner. One day I went
home when he was there and my mother told him I'd won a
race the day before at the school sports. He looked very gravely
at me for a few minutes without speaking. Then: 'Best runner
in the class, were you, boy?' I nodded. 'And do you like
running?' I nodded again. The corners of his mouth twitched

into a very faint smile. 'Keep it up, boy . . . it's always handy to be able to run.'

My grandpa was always so prosperous-looking, which is the only thing that counts with children, that for a long time I was sure he must be a business man, especially as when he was leaving he often said: 'Well, I must be getting off to the City.'

About the only other thing I knew about him was he often went to 'The Races'. I knew this was something that gentlemen did, and used to imagine him like the people I'd seen in films, moving about in the fashionable crowds with a big cigar and binoculars.

Actually, I was right—that was just what he did do—but I didn't know what for, until one day I found him at our house on his own, Mother being out. Scattered all over the table were watches and purses—what looked like hundreds of them to me as a child. Grandpa was passing the time waiting for my mother by counting up his day's haul. When I came in he very slowly gathered them all together and packed them away in a canvas hold-all. When he'd finished he fastened it up carefully, took up his gloves, his cane, and his hat from the table, and turned to go. At the door he stopped and looked back at me. 'Still doing your running, boy?' I nodded. He nodded back, seriously. 'That's right, boy. You keep it up.'

He must have been a good pickpocket, because he only had one good arm and hand. I've got the idea he used the other one as a blind, something to focus people's attention on while he dipped them. Like all good thieves he worked regularly, using his appearance to advantage both at the races and in the City. And, like all pickpockets, he was fearless on the job. Unlike many of them, though, he was also fearless off it, and was forever telling people what he thought about them, usually critically. I suppose nobody whacked him because of his arm. Diplomacy was the one thing he couldn't be accused of, and

he handed out opinions and advice to everyone he met. Looking back, I know he was nothing but a puffed-up bag of wind;
but when I was a kid I thought he was some sort of oracle.
He even used to make me think Leyton Orient were a great
team, the way he talked about them. Leyton Orient! He'd
have made a good con-man even if the pocket-picking business
had folded up.

My father didn't like him, which he knew, and that was
why he only came round to see my mother during the daytime.
She didn't approve of him either, but as he was her father and
she was a bit scared of him she had to put up with him. It
wasn't so much him being a thief my father disliked, as the
fact he always tried to look as though he belonged to a better
class than his own. This was the worst crime of all to my old
man, denying your origins: it was worse even than indifference
to the iniquities of the capitalist system.

'The System' both fascinated and repelled my father.
He was always getting books on economics out of the library,
trying to learn how society worked: and when he found out
he fumed and raged and argued about it bitterly with anyone
who'd listen. I remember one time he had some text of
a company's regulations, or something, which referred to
workers as 'servants of the company', and he went on about it
for hours to my mother.

He always had a great sense of solidarity with other men
working with him, and it wasn't just theoretical. Often I'd
hear him telling my mother to make up his sandwiches for the
day in two lots. Sometimes she'd try to argue with him about it,
but he'd say sharply: 'Shut up and do as I say.' There was
some man on the job who hadn't got enough to eat, and my
father was going to see he had something, even if his own were
cut in half. But it was never to earn himself gratitude, only
because he felt all the workers should stand together. I once
saw him stick a ten-bob note in a man's top pocket in the

street outside. He didn't know I was behind him; and when the man started to argue my father said: 'Cop that and bugger off,' and walked away.

His generosity must have been a strain on my mother, seeing him give things away when we were so short ourselves, but I never heard her complain. She wasn't very brainy, but she was philosophical and she loved my father: her whole life was centred on him and their kids. Poverty, hunger, worry, hurt—these were the only things she knew about, and she never asked for anything different. Because she knew that my father loved her; that was all that really mattered to her. He was very conscious of the fact he hadn't done well enough by her, and used to say often if there was any justice in the world one day she'd have all the things she wanted. But they both knew there wasn't, and would never be. To this day I still don't understand why he never went thieving to get her some of the things she ought to have had in life.

My mother was the first person I ever stole from, the first person I ever hurt. The recollection of it's dim, so I must have been very young, four perhaps or five at the most. I came in and saw a two-shilling piece lying on the table. She was out of the room, and I slipped it into my pocket and went out again. I went down to the corner shop and bought sweets and ice-cream; there were some other kids hanging about on the corner as usual, so I treated them to ice-cream as well. When they thanked me I felt terrific. By the time I got back home the sweets were all gone, and I'd forgotten I'd done anything.

My mother was sitting at the table with her face in her hands, crying. When I asked her what was up, she said: 'I've gone and lost another two bob, it was all I'd got left for the rest of the week.' She was always losing things, so it never crossed her mind I'd taken it.

I went downstairs and out to the lavatory in the yard and shut myself in. I knew I'd done wrong and hurt someone, and I knew I ought to be hurt in return. I clenched my fists up and beat them on the lavatory wall until the knuckles were bleeding and the pain was making me cry. Then I ran out into the street, and I didn't go home until it was dark.

When I got back she saw my hands and asked me what had happened. I said I'd fallen on a pile of bricks and she got hot water and bathed them to make them better. Then she gave me a drink of tea and put me to bed, making a fuss of me because I'd hurt myself. By the next day, of course, she'd forgotten all about losing the money.

But I hadn't. Not by the next day or the next week or the next year. The guilt of it followed me all the time, and years later I was still trying to cancel it out. If I collected pennies for Guy Fawkes, I gave them to her; when I went out selling bits of wood to neighbours for their fires, I did the same. But she always used to make me keep the money and, what was much worse, whenever I did it she told people about it, saying how good I was, how kind and generous and always trying to help my mother.

I never did get up enough courage to tell her the truth— that I wasn't good but guilty, and was trying to expiate, and never could because of the kindness and thanks she gave in return. For the rest of her life I kept this feeling, and still have it, it still worries me vaguely even now. I never stole from her again.

Naturally I had to spend part of my life at school, but it was as little as I could make it, because I didn't like it. I truanted far more than I attended. Subjects like history and geography were all right, and I enjoyed running and boxing and other sports. But the big trouble was school meant obedience to authority, and this is something I've never taken to. They tried to get this into me more than any subject on the curriculum, but it didn't work. Punishments made no difference, whatever sort they were, beatings or anything else.

One teacher had the bright idea once of punishing me for some misdemeanour by making me sit with the girls. She didn't know it, but she was doing me a favour because I was a lecherous little bastard even then, and I enjoyed reefing girls much more than lessons. The girls enjoyed it too, and I used to misbehave deliberately afterwards with that teacher so I'd get put with them. In those days a lot of girls had little pockets in their knickers where they kept their ha'pennies for milk money. I found out that while I was giving them a thrill by reefing them I could nick their cash at the same time, and they couldn't very well complain about it afterwards to the teacher because she'd have wanted to know what they were doing letting me put my hand in their knickers. So I discovered at an early age the definition of an ideal life—doing something that gets you kicks and money at the same time.

But the school's usual idea of punishment was the old English perversion of beating. There were times I was whacked so hard I could feel the weals on my arse like corrugated cardboard. One woman teacher gave it me for throwing a board-duster, and her system was that you had to say, in between each stroke: 'I will not throw board-dusters,' or whatever you'd done. I wouldn't say it, so she kept hitting harder each time to try and make me, but I still wouldn't. Exasperated, she grabbed at my belt and tried to pull my pants down so she could beat me on my bare flesh. To do that, she had to put the cane down, and I picked it up and slashed at her with it until her screaming brought one of the masters running in.

The punishment the headmaster decided on for that was twenty-four stripes laid on in front of the whole school. At least he didn't try to take my trousers off, so I just gritted my

C

teeth and thought damn them all, and eventually it was over.

Afterwards I went out into the bicycle shed, found the bike of the woman teacher and slashed her tyres to ribbons, and then I went back inside to the cloakrooms with a lump of old iron I'd found and smashed up the sinks.

That was how I was then, and I've not changed much. When someone acts primitively towards you, you act primitively back, on the same level as you're treated. Attempting to destroy something that is part of me—however unpleasant or reprehensible a characteristic it is—only makes me want to destroy something of authority's in return.

I should think the product I am today ought to prove thrashings are no good, and only produce responses of vengeance and violence. It makes me laugh when I read of the Tory women at Bournemouth calling for a return of the cat. Even on what you might call simply an economic basis, I and all the people I know would prefer the cat to a long sentence any time. After three days it doesn't hurt any more, and the scars soon heal, except those on your mind. What you feel is anger, resentment, and, most of all, a determination somehow to get your own back. But being deterred? The idea never gets a look in.

The only thing that gets anywhere at all is kindness. It might not get far, but it's got much more chance than anything else. I'd like to make it clear, though, that this isn't an appeal for kindness in dealing with criminals. I think kindness is probably better for the people who are handing it out, but that's all. As a criminal myself, it's a matter of indifference to me whether I'm treated kindly or cruelly, and neither will change me. For others—well, with kindness there is always the faint hope they might respond: but anyone who responds to ill-treatment and brutality must be solid from the neck up.

My mother whacked me regularly. Sometimes I deserved

it, but I always knew when she did it she meant it for the best. The school beatings were different, because there people were trying to terrify me into obedience. They didn't succeed, but they did build up my standing with the other kids, and make me into no end of a hero and tough-guy and what followed on naturally from that: being a bully.

There was one kid there who I noticed soon after he first came. He was undersized, quiet, nervous, and Jewish. You can't start out on life with more strikes against you than that. One day, just to show how important I was, I stopped one of the other kids from giving him a beating. From then on Izzy was always following me around, giving me bags of broken sweets which he brought from his mother's shop. Somehow or other we struck up a friendship. Since he was physically weak and I was a bully, that suited him. He had a bright, inquiring mind and I was stupid, so that fascinated me. We used to play truant together, going off down to the docks and watching the ships in the river. But Izzy was never satisfied to leave it at that. He made notes of the colours of their flags, and then we had to go to the library and look them up to find out where they came from.

When we were in school, he was always standing up in class and asking ridiculous questions like 'Why is the sky blue?' and 'Why does the British Army do all its defending by fighting in other people's countries?' and similar things the teachers couldn't answer. I used to sit and watch him with my mouth open, wondering how he ever thought things like that up. I learnt far more from him than I did from teachers, whose only idea was to cram the three R's into you and get back home quick when it was four o'clock. It wasn't knowledge, but something better: how to take an interest in things, how to find out about things that interest you, how to make journeys and explorations without moving a foot.

I learnt other things from friendship with Izzy too. His

grandmother had a shop as well as his mother, a second-hand-clothing shop in the Mile End Road. One night the Blackshirts smashed in the windows and chucked dirt and rubbish on the clothes. Up till then I'd always thought they were rather heroic, the Blackshirts, when I'd seen them marching around in their get-up with bands and banners. I'd no idea what they were about, but anything showy like that appeals to a kid.

When Izzy told me about his grandma's shop, and was crying about it, I knew what they were—a lousy bunch of bastards. I knew he was expecting me to suggest we did something about it, too. So the next night I took him up to the market. We got a barrow and some straw, and trundled it off to the Blackshirt meeting room in the next street. It was in the basement of a bakery and there was no one there, just an empty room with a big trestle table and a couple of forms. We piled up the straw in the middle of the room, and set fire to it. It was damp and didn't burn, and we were scared anyway so we didn't stop. All it did was make a bit of smoke, and it can't have caused much trouble to put out. We were only eight or nine at the time and there was nothing much two kids could do. But at least we did try, and of course it was the only way we knew to answer violence: with violence back again.

That was always axiomatic. If somebody sloshed you, you sloshed him: if you weren't big enough, you got somebody else to do it for you. It was as much part of everyday life and behaviour as the houses, was violence.

The first time I saw it really seriously I was a bit scared, but it never occurred to me to think it anything unusual. I was playing in the street with a kid called Billy O'Lynn when his mother came out of the house and said to him: 'Go up to the Devonshire and tell your father there's some men want to see him in Island Street. And give him this.'

'This' was a bundle of rags. As soon as we got round the corner we opened it, and there was a shooter inside. We wrapped it up again and took it to his father in the Devonshire, with the message, and we saw him come out a few minutes later and start walking up towards Island Street.

We followed him, keeping out of sight in case he looked round, and went through the back yards of some houses along Island Street itself, until we found a shed roof to climb up on where we could watch. There were some men waiting for him at a corner, and when he got near them they started to fan out across the road. He pulled out the shooter and banged away, and they all ran off up the street, piling into a car and driving away fast.

He came walking back down the street again, and saw us up on the shed roof. His face was red and twisted up with the tension. He looked at us for a minute, then he shouted out: 'If any bastards ever come after you, you treat 'em like that, don't wait till they come for you.' He didn't say it as though he was showing off or trying to impress us, just spat the words out, full of hatred, and then walked off slowly down the street. An odd thing is that Billy O'Lynn grew up to be a dead-straight kid.

The other thing that was normal as well as violence was people going to prison. I don't recall when I first heard it mentioned, but it must have been about the same time I heard words like' money' and 'food'. 'Prison' was basic in any child's vocabulary, and there was never any reluctance about mentioning it. The idea of a child being taunted by his schoolmates, for instance, because his father was in jail, would have been ludicrous. It was an everyday thing that sometimes happened to people: they went to prison, then they came back. It was hard luck, but it was the sort of thing that happened when you got caught for something by the Law. You might just as well have tried to taunt a schoolmate with something like 'It's

37

raining'. He'd turn round and say: 'So what, I know it's raining.'

Another friend at school was a kid called 'Pancho' Delaney. I've forgotten his real name: he was never called anything else but 'Pancho'. He had God's greatest gift to a criminal, an honest face, and because of this he was always being put in positions of trust at school, helping to collect money for milk and things like that. I teamed up with him early on in a very good partnership: I thought up the schemes and he carried them out. When the discovery came, he stood up with his fresh features and his clear blue eyes and said: 'Honestly, sir, it was all there when I counted it.' He usually got away with it.

All in all, the time I spent at school was educational in many ways, even if they weren't all strictly academic. For instance I broadened my experience with girls. By the time I was ten or eleven I was having regular screws, usually with girls of the same age but sometimes a bit older. The first time was in a costermonger's yard with a girl of ten who was in the same school class. It wasn't very successful or enjoyable, but it gave me the taste for it and I persisted until it was. Lots of the girls were just as keen on it as I was. Of course if I'd had a good education and gone to a posh boarding school I wouldn't have gone in for filthy things like that. I'd have been a decent little homosexual instead.

I got a fractured skull when I was ten. My father must have been working at the time, because my mother gave me a pound note to go and get changed at the Devonshire. I ran across the road and was hit by a car, and the next I knew I was in hospital with my head in bandages, down in the X-ray room, a huge place full of lights and pipes and machines which frightened me sick.

When I got better I was sent away for convalescence to a home at Margate or Hastings, somewhere like that. This was the first time in my life I'd ever been to the seaside, but I was too lonely and homesick to enjoy it. All I wanted was to get back.

Before that happened there was a mix-up which did nothing to increase my liking for the authorities. My mother had been sent a letter telling her to collect me on a certain day at County Hall. Two days before I was due to go the convalescent home thought it was having an epidemic of scarlet fever, so my mother was sent a letter saying not to collect me as I couldn't be returned. The day after, they found out it wasn't scarlet fever after all, so off went yet another letter saying I was going to be at County Hall as originally arranged.

She must have been out or something, because she didn't get it. I was sitting at County Hall with all the other kids who'd been brought back, and one by one they were collected by their parents. When it got to half past five and I was the only one left, it was decided to board me out for the night. Why they couldn't have taken me home I'll never know, but of course I was too young to argue about it. When you're a kid you think grown-ups know what they're doing, and anyway the ones at County Hall aren't exactly approachable.

I was taken to a children's home. To say it was like a prison would be flattery. In all my life I've never heard people talk with such desperation about escaping as the people there did —and those people were children, kids like myself. They were there for a lot longer than I was, although I didn't know that at the time, nobody having thought it worth while to tell me. I was just put there and left, feeling that somehow, like a package in the post, I'd been mislaid.

All the time without a single let-up it was sit still, don't talk, stand up, do this, go there, sit down, eat that, drink this, go and have a crap, stand there, sit down, keep quiet. In between there were constant whacks on the neck with rulers for not eating, eating too much, talking, not talking: it never mattered, whatever you were doing was wrong. Next morning my mother

39

turned up, and it was all over. But only for me. I didn't forget the other kids there for a long time. Ever since, nothing's ever happened to me that seemed as horrible and frightening as that.

I always knew that stealing was wrong, or at least, like swearing, it wasn't the thing to do. I learned this early on when I went home one day with two eggs I'd pinched from a stall in the market, and my mother marched me back there and made me hand them over to the stallholder. All the kids stole: comics from outside paper-shops, fruit, vegetables, sweets—anything they could. It wasn't so much necessity as habit, really, and although it was known to be wrong it wasn't a very important wrong. If you fancied something, but had no money, you tried to pinch it. Even if you had money you still tried to pinch it, because it saved your money for spending on something else. You also pinched things that were lying around, because they were asking to be pinched; and anyway if you didn't do it somebody else would.

This was the code. Nobody argued about it, or even discussed it. It had existed long before we were born and we grew up with it and into it.

Some kids were actively encouraged by their parents to do it, others got beaten when they were caught. But the operative part was the last four words—'when they were caught'. Being beaten was a reason for not being caught; never a reason for not stealing. Being beaten simply taught you to be more careful. That was what you had to learn, and the only way of learning it was by painful experience of what happened to you when you were caught.

Every time I was caught I was thrashed, usually with a hair-brush, sometimes with a belt. When I read of people like magistrates telling someone what he needs is a good thrashing,

I often wonder if they know how many he's had already. What makes them think one more will make any difference?

About the only places I never stole from were the second-hand-book shops. There were quite a few of them round the market. They may not have been exactly Bumpus' or Foyle's, but to me they were fascinating places that I was always browsing around. For some reason the men who kept them never objected to a scruffy, dirty-fingered kid pawing their books, spending hours looking at things which he obviously hadn't the money to buy. Some of them gave me books sometimes, usually old ones they'd given up hope of selling—great, thick tomes with steel-engravings, on subjects like biblical history or anthropology. I used to take them home and polish the covers with boot polish till they glowed, and then put them up on a cupboard shelf, or under my bed. I was always determined that some day I was going to read them, in the near future when I had time. But the near future was always the never-present.

I did read one or two which were sufficiently interesting to grip me straight away, usually the ones on history or geography. But reading was never easy at home because of the number of people and the shortage of quiet and space. By the side of one of the fireplaces there was a tall cupboard with large cracks in its doors. I found that if I got inside and shut the doors no one would disturb me, and there was sufficient light coming in through the cracks for me to see by. I spent a lot of time in there, especially in winter because it was warm. Sometimes I fell asleep, and my father would lift me out when he remembered I was still there, and put me into bed. He was pleased, always, when he found me reading, and encouraged me to keep it up. He brought books home from the library for me, things far above my head by people like Robert Blatchford and William Morris, saying: 'Read that, son, it'll tell you a lot of things you ought to know about.'

But I wasn't old enough, and I didn't understand them: sometimes, in fact, I was almost physically afraid of them. I remember one in particular whose title, because it looked so strange and terrifying, nearly gave me nightmares just to look at it. It was called *The Ragged Trousered Philanthropists*. It's strange that when I did come to read it, much later in life, it knocked me sideways. I've never read a book, before or since, which made such a profound impression on me, and I still think it's one of the greatest books that's ever been written.

I couldn't read my father's books, but my rebelliousness against things as they were was growing without any help from him. I don't know what began the process: all I know is that I always seemed to have it, almost from a natural instinct.

And I wasn't a conventionally deprived child either. I had a mother and father who loved each other and got on well, and loved and were loved by their children. If I put it down to poverty I think it would be true, or at least more true than anything else I can think of. But it wouldn't be true to say that an environment of poverty makes everyone a criminal, because it doesn't. There were plenty of people—or there were some people—who came from just the same surroundings that I did, who grew up straight: Billy O'Lynn, for instance. But poverty, I suppose, does different things to different people; and in my case I think it was the major factor in my becoming a criminal.

What are usually called the working classes are basically animal. Strength, the ability to overcome conditions, is the most important thing: and it brings with it greed and possessiveness. The greed isn't purely avaricious: it's more a desire for things you haven't got but feel you've a right to, because other people have them—a sharp suit, good things, neat things, flashy things; all the trappings of position and importance.

And in this class love, too, is a different sort of thing, a more basic thing, than that more generally understood. A parent gives his child a thrashing, but he still loves it and feels

42

part of it and feels it is part of him, in a way parents who put their kids out to boarding schools can never do.

And in this class the unreal things of life—by which I mean non-useful things like the arts, music, and so on—don't matter, they don't even exist except just as vague happenings on the horizon. If people have only a few facets of character they tend to be more intensified: if they have no interests beyond their own human nature their nature is more fundamental, and their life is governed almost entirely by experiences and feelings. The confines are narrow, but they're very deep.

Am I saying what I mean, am I getting over what I'm trying to say? I don't think I am, I'll try again. . . .

I made up my mind almost as early as I can remember that poverty was not going to be for me. As a child, to me poverty was a crime: the nastiest crime in the world. Imagine the foullest, most repugnant deed you can think of, and then change the image to poverty. That was what it meant to me: that was how I felt about it—as something soul-destroying and foul, something dirtying and full of shame, something that cut into me and seared through me and filled me full of hate.

It became like this quite clearly one particular day. I'd wandered out of my own streets, exploring, and suddenly found myself in a big road lined on each side with towering buildings, full of the noise of traffic and people. It was new, frightening, overwhelming. I didn't know it then, but its name was Bishopsgate.

I was standing on the pavement, gawping up at these buildings that looked like monsters—and suddenly I heard people laughing behind me, and I turned round. A group of men, City workers, well dressed in smart suits, were pointing at me. Because my arse was showing through a big hole in the seat of my pants.

I backed up against the wall of one of the buildings, a bank I think it was, and stood there feeling the cold of the stone as my arse pressed against it, trying to pull down my jersey to cover

43

the hole. I knew I must move, and I was afraid to. It seemed I was there hours, trapped like an animal, until they went away.

And then I ran. Twisting through the side alleys and the courtyards, feeling ashamed and sick and defiled. Climbing over walls, dodging through yards, anything to avoid having to go back on the main road. And suddenly I found myself in Spitalfields, and I could relax . . . because there I was among my own people again, who were as poor as I was, whose fun was good-natured fun, who could shout out: 'Oi! Your arse is showing, mate,' without it having any malice in it at all. I could laugh at that, and give back an answer in street-arab repartee, because it was meant kindly and was only fun. But when others did it, of a better class and a better social standing, it wasn't funny. It hurt and brought shame.

But of all things there was one I hated even more than ridicule, and that was pity: the pity of the charitable who give to the poor. This hobby of giving cast-offs to the poor is dying out these days: now people send their old clothes to the Oxford Committee for Famine Relief or something like that, and get back a voucher to say what good people they are. But it's like playing chess by post, it leaves a lot to be desired. They miss the pleasure of handing out the stuff themselves, like the people used to do down at the Mission Hall.

They came in their cars, these women, gracious and benevolent, giving what they didn't want to the needy poor. Perhaps they were good people at heart: but the social system that put them, and us, in that position was wrong. We took the clothes they gave, and we were ungrateful. And we were not only ungrateful, we went further, we hated the people who did the giving, hated the necessity that made us accept them instead of throwing them back in their faces—their thin, aquiline, fine-boned faces with their delicate skins and their sensitive mouths, that showed the same good breeding you get in racehorses. Only I like racehorses. And the sweet, good-looking girls of nineteen and twenty who came too, with their terribly tactful manner and their jolly, friendly voices, and the laughter that came so easily to prove how unstuck-up they were. . . . It was disgusting and it was obscene, and to be part of it, to be a person it happened to, because of how one was born and how one lived, this was the most disgusting and obscene thing of all.

With poverty it isn't just one thing etching itself into the mind, it's a hundred, a thousand, it's everything. As a sailor adopts the ways of the sea in his walk and his talk, in his gestures and actions and mannerisms of speech, so an environment of poverty afflicts the whole appearance and character of those who grow up in it. The pattern colours everything, all actions and thoughts and responses; fills every nook and cranny of you, leaving no room anywhere for anything else.

It didn't matter in those days to poor people that the King was reviewing the fleet at Spithead, that the Royal Academy was holding its annual exhibition at Burlington House, that British colonial policy wasn't all it ought to be. It didn't matter that Sir Malcolm Campbell had broken the world's land speed record or there was civil war in Spain. All that did matter was there was never quite enough to eat, that work was hard to find, that clothes were thin and roofs let in the rain. There was no time for anything else but poverty and what it was like.

And from a very early age, as soon as I could think about things and understand things and react to them, I made up my mind that poverty was not going to be for me.

By the time I was twelve I'd more or less stopped going to school, except on odd occasions when it couldn't be avoided. There was a shortage of schools that would put up with me too: those that had had me weren't keen to make me come back, and those that hadn't were not keen to take me on. My father didn't press it because he thought the whole educational system was lousy anyway, his ideas being more along the lines of A. S. Neill. From what I've read since about his schools, they might have suited me. I doubt whether they'd have changed me, but I'd certainly have fitted in with the thieving, smashing things up, smoking, and all the rest of it.

When the war started the LCC began a big scheme of evacuating schoolchildren, and somehow my name got on their list. My mother and father thought it was a good idea, so I was packed off with the others to somewhere in Buckinghamshire, ending up late in the day in a school hall waiting for some kind local inhabitant to offer us a home. It was rather like a cattle market where people came along to pick out the best-looking beasts. My brother and I stood side by side waiting for someone to fancy us, but time went on and nobody did. Him they'd take on his own, yes, because he was an attractive, cheerful-looking sort of kid: but he wouldn't part from me, and there was something about me that prospective buyers didn't fancy. Perhaps it was because I was smoking, swearing, and generally being noisy and showing off.

Eventually the woman who was organizing the reception realized she was going to be stuck with us herself, so she took us off to her home and pitched us in with her own family. They were very nice, but Salvation Army with all the trimmings— uniform, going to the Citadel, prayers at the drop of a hat— and I hated it.

After two days my mother sent us a postal order for pocket money, and it was just enough for the train fare back to London for one. I told my brother to hang on, hopped off home and told Mum we didn't like it, and she got us back. The bombing hadn't started, so there seemed no reason for us to be away. Life went on again as before, but with even less reason now for going to school.

I spent most of my time enjoying myself and getting into

trouble, but there was never anything very serious about it. My mother and father plugged away at me with hidings or ruckings whenever I got too out of hand, doing their best with a mixture of love and punishment to get me to behave. It was about this time I began to think hard about my father, and work out in my own mind that his arguments about the right way to live were, to say the least, academic ones, and certainly didn't get him any benefits.

Then after a while the bombing began, and once more children were evacuated. This time we were sent off to Devon, and my brother and I went to live on a farm. The farmer's wife was a lovely woman, kind and gentle, and for the first couple of weeks I really enjoyed myself. The air was fresh and the food was good. I even began to get around to the idea that perhaps I might try going back to school. She introduced it very gradually and I think might eventually have got me to do it.

But one morning she got a letter, and I could see from the writing it was from my father. In the middle of reading it she burst out crying, and I knew what it said. We'd heard that the bombing was really very bad, much worse than they let on in the papers or on the wireless, so I suppose I was half expecting it. 'It's my mum, isn't it?' I said. She just nodded, looking at me helplessly and going on crying. My brother came into the kitchen, and he knew, too, without anybody saying anything, and he started to cry as well. I grabbed him by the shoulders and shook him and said: 'Shut up, you bloody great baby,' and then I ran out into the field at the back.

I wasn't going to let anybody see me cry, but it wasn't bravery, just the hopelessness of it all. What could a child do? A man could swear he'd have revenge and go off and join up and fight, but I couldn't. There was only one thing to do: not let anyone see how much it mattered.

She was, I think, the only really important person in my life. She was the one I had to answer to, feel sorry at hurting,

47

face when I'd done wrong. With her death, I was free of all that, but it wasn't a freedom I was glad of all the same. Now nothing mattered. There was no one who'd be hurt by what I did.

I'd like to be able to say that if she hadn't died things might have been different, I might not have turned out as I did. But I don't think it's true. She'd have put up a hell of a fight about my taking to crime, I know that, and she's the only person I would have paid any attention to. But I won't pretend she might have won, because I don't think she would.

Anyway, it's irrelevant now. She did die, and that was that. She was scatter-brained, not very bright, not very clever. But she loved me, she cared about what I was doing, what I felt, what I thought: she always respected me as a person in my own right. However much she thrashed me when I was small, which was a lot, she always loved me and I always knew she did. And then she went, and that was that.

We came back to London because my father wanted to be near his children. He was on war work in a factory, and it was funny that from then on he stayed in work and money got less tight. Years afterwards he used to say: 'If only Mum had lived just a little bit longer, she'd have seen us turn the corner and had a few things for herself as well.'

Naturally he couldn't look after us all, so we were parked out with various friends and relatives. I was put with my aunt, one of his sisters. Why she ever said she'd have me I don't know: I think it can only have been because he was paying her for it. Of all the horrible, mean bastards I've ever met, my Aunt May took the prize.

Physically she was a handsome woman, running a bit to fat, perhaps, and always over-dressed. She thought she was at least two cuts above everyone else and married a man with a 'decent' job, not a common labourer but a clerk. The fact he was an outright twerp and very poorly paid didn't matter: at

48

least he wore a white collar and wasn't common like the rest of us.

She treated me exactly like a paying lodger, with the difference that for any other paying lodger she'd have had to do at least something. I was left to get my own food, do my own washing and mending, and get on as best I could without help of any kind. As I was just over thirteen, it wasn't easy. She was always out, usually drinking in the local at night or working in a factory during the day, and often she'd go away for a couple of days at the week-end without even bothering to mention she was going.

I got a job as general runabout and tea-maker in a little hardware shop in Stepney, owned by an elderly man and his wife, who were kind people even though they hadn't much money, and used to ask me to their home to stay when they knew I was going to be on my own at my aunt's. They got keen on the idea of adopting me, and training me to manage the shop for them after the war.

They started me off at 22s. 6d. a week, of which my aunt took a pound for my keep. The old man soon saw that I wasn't eating at all during the day while I was working for him. When I told him why, he put my pay up straight away by 5s. I was very proud of getting this rise, and told my aunt. She said it was very lucky because she'd just been working out that keeping me was costing her 25s. a week, and if I hadn't been able to pay another five bob she'd have had to ask me to go.

My father had been moved up to the Midlands under a Direction of Labour order, and he had to spend most of his spare time and money travelling about seeing my younger brothers and sisters who were scattered round other members of the family. He felt because I was the eldest, and was working, that I could fend for myself better than the others, so I didn't see a lot of him. I was very unhappy, and I couldn't see much hope of the future getting any brighter.

It came to Christmas and my aunt announced she was going away again for a few days. Her parting words as she went out on the morning of Christmas Eve were: 'Now you won't make a filthy mess everywhere, will you?' and then she went. No suggestions about what I should do for Christmas, no presents, nothing. Not even a jar of shrimp-paste for Christmas dinner. Just: 'Don't make a mess.'

Christmas Eve I was walking along the street, wondering what I was going to do, when I ran into Pancho. When I told him how I was fixed he suggested we should clean the house out and go up to Oldham for Christmas, where he said he had some friends, and have a good time for a few days.

We went back to my aunt's together. At first all we could find was 5s. 3d. in an old jam-jar where she kept threepenny bits, and a book of savings certificates which were no good because we couldn't cash them. While I was up in her bedroom turning out the drawers to see if I could find anything else, I heard a terrific clanging downstairs and went down to see Pancho getting stuck into the gas meter with an iron bar. There was a pound or two in there, so then we opened the electric meter as well, which also had a bit in it. After that we both felt scared and decided to go on our way. As we were going out I told him to wait a minute. I went back and took the savings certificates, because if they were no good to us at least she wouldn't have the benefit of them.

I'd no idea where Oldham was, and I don't think Pancho had either. He did the ticket-buying at the railway station and off we went, at night on a war-time train journey, stopping and starting for hour after hour like train journeys were in those times. We ended up in the early hours of Christmas morning at Crewe, wandering about the streets trying to find somewhere to get a cup of tea. But we couldn't find anywhere open, and finally went into a bus shelter and dropped off to sleep.

We were woken up by a policeman and taken to the police station, where we stayed all Christmas Day while they tried to find out who we were and where we'd come from, and where they could send us back to. Gradually it all came out. They phoned the Stepney police, who got hold of my aunt, and then we were taken back to London and charged. We knew the meter business was serious. This, for the first time in my life, was real crime.

People often say it's how someone is dealt with the first time that really matters, and makes all the difference as to whether they go straight or not. It depends on who's being dealt with, I suppose. I don't think my case will be much help to that school of thought.

My feelings when I was brought up in court were a mixture of fear and resentment, with a lot of embarrassment at being the centrepiece whom everyone was looking at and talking about. I didn't understand what was happening, and I was worried about what was going to happen. Pancho already had a bit of a record, so he was shipped straight off to approved school, leaving me on my own, up in front of Basil Henriques.

I have met people who wouldn't have anything good about him, naturally, but he made a terrific impression on me. I thought he was exceptionally kind, a wonderful man, considerate and most anxious to get at the truth. He'd got none of the usual air of judicial indifference that never breaks except into viciousness, and he did everything he could to put me at ease. He looked concerned, he sounded concerned, and he gave me all the time I wanted, without pushing me, to explain why I'd done what I had. First of all he let my aunt tell her side of the story, how she'd done everything for me and how ungrateful I was. Then he asked me.

I told him about the wages and the rise, about her keeping me short of money and food, about her going off and leaving me all the time. I told him how I felt about her, what I thought of her, why I didn't feel sorry or ashamed for what I'd done. Half-way through, I suddenly realized I'd won. I'd won because he was listening; I'd won because what I was saying was true and he was recognizing it; because he was paying attention to what a child said instead of automatically believing an adult.

He made a short speech and he hit hard. He said she was encouraging me to be a criminal by not giving me enough attention and by keeping me short of things I needed so I almost had to steal. When she said she wasn't going to take me back he said he hadn't proposed sending me back, because it wasn't good for me to be with her. I needed looking after if I wasn't going to get into really serious trouble. When I stood up in front of him again at the end he looked at me very sternly, but there was kindness and feeling in his face.

He said: 'I'm going to bind you over to be of good behaviour for twelve months, and I'm going to make arrangements for you to live in a hostel where you'll be properly looked after. I don't want you to leave here feeling that you're now a criminal, because you're not. It's what you do from now that will decide whether you become one. So forget all about it and have a fresh start, and I shall be making regular inquiries to see how you're getting on.'

That a man in his position should talk to me like that, behave to me like that, made me feel great. He didn't think I was a criminal and neither did I. Even if I'd chopped my aunt in little pieces I still wouldn't have done. He'd weighed it all up and come down on my side, and he was giving me a chance.

I suppose this is the point where I ought to look back and say: 'Ah, if I'd only listened to him . . .' Well, I don't. He did give me a chance and I admire him for it, because I think it was the right thing to do with any kid. It certainly wasn't his fault that in my case it didn't work. He tried.

A probation officer took me to the hostel. On the way he

said: 'Use your loaf and behave yourself and you'll be O.K.'
It was a big Victorian house, run by the Church Army, with
about thirty boys in it. They weren't all there for doing something wrong, some of them were just orphans, and it was run
by a tubby middle-aged bloke in a green tweed suit. Officially
that is; actually it was run by two of the older boys, about
eighteen—pipe-smoking, lordly types with superior breeding
and inferior brains who thought they'd inherited the privilege
of telling other people what to do.

The second night I was there we had an argument over
whose turn it was at billiards. One of them started laying down
the law to me, poking me in the chest with the stem of his
pipe. I had a cue in my hand, so I poked him right back in
the face with that, and there was a right rumpus all round,
with everyone joining in.

The next morning I looked out of the window after breakfast and there, hanging about in the street and trying to see
what was going on inside the hostel, was Pancho. I slipped
out.

'What's it like?' he said.

'Rotten,' I said. 'What's your approved school like?'

'Rotten,' he said. 'I've scarpered. What about jacking up
together?'

'Sure,' I said.

So we did.

I didn't go back inside the hostel, just walked off with him
down the street. Two days is a long time when you're young—
quite long enough for me to have forgotten what old Henriques
had said. I don't think it even crossed my mind.

We had to find somewhere for me to live. Pancho was all
right because he was back with his family, but he told me he
knew an old bombed-out pub near their place, which he thought
would suit me fine. We went along to have a look. All that was
left standing of it was two walls, a bit of staircase, half of the

53

first floor, and a slice of roof. Pancho promised to keep me fed, and I moved in. The whole area round about had been knocked flat, so there weren't many people about to worry us.

It worked fine. During the day I went off to the markets, Spitalfields or Billingsgate, doing odd jobs like helping with the loading, or pushing barrows for the porters, earning tips and scrounging a bit of food on the side.

The pub was a cold place to sleep, so I used to walk round the streets at night until I was really knocked up and could just fall asleep when I got back, under the staircase on a pile of old rags and bits of curtain. Some nights I couldn't get to sleep, however tired I was, because of the air-raids, which were pretty bad, and I used to crawl up the staircase, keeping close to the wall for safety, and get up to the first floor where I could lie watching the fires and the searchlights, the bursts of anti-aircraft shells, and the moon. It was like watching a film and seemed to have nothing to do with me at all. Other times, when a bomb fell close, I'd get scared to death and crawl back under the stairs to my hiding place, covering myself up and shivering with cold and fright.

I'd get a sudden wild fear that the pub was going to be hit again, and I'd be buried under the rubble with no one knowing I was there. Perhaps years later when they were clearing up the debris they'd come across a dirty skeleton under the stairs, all that was left of what once had been me. Then when the daylight came I'd realize I'd survived, and back I'd climb again up the staircase on to the floor above, looking out over the roofs of the city, seeing the dust and the clouds of smoke.

One of the walls was a big one covered with plain white wallpaper, and I used to write over it with bits of charred wood I'd found, scribbling away in the early hours of the morning until it was safe to go out. I wrote whatever I could think of, usually in lists—names of ships, titles of books, kinds of insects, my favourite foods, heroes, dogs' names, anything. After air-

54

raids when I'd been frightened I'd write in great looping letters right across the wall: '*You bloody German bastards,*' '*Hitler, I hope your balls drop off* ', and similar things that expressed my feelings. It was my first venture into literature.

I was sure the entire police force of London must be looking for me because I'd run away from the hostel, and I was sure, too, that anyone who knew me and caught sight of me would probably tip them off. In a way there was something exciting and heroic as well as frightening about it, like a bandit living in a cave. On top of that, Hitler and his lot were trying to blow me to bits—so I had two sets of enemies. They may have been fighting each other but one thing they had in common was that they were both out to get me.

All I had to fight them with, growing stronger every night in the cold, dark loneliness of the shell of the pub, was a determination that they bloody well weren't going to succeed. Somehow I was going to get through, without getting caught and without being killed. I knew from books that somehow the outlaw always did.

2

The Outlaw Becomes a Criminal

Wʜᴇɴ bits started to fall off the pub during the air-raids, I realized it wasn't going to need a direct hit to bring the whole lot down on top of me. Pancho said he knew of an empty street shelter which no one used because it was in a road that had been completely flattened. I moved in there, and we furnished it with odds and ends of chairs that we found in bombed-out houses, and got it quite comfortable.

There was only one snag. Officially the shelter was disused, and the door was fastened with a big padlock. Sometimes the police came round checking. So every night, with a suitable key we'd found, Pancho locked me in and came back early in the morning to let me out. I started to worry. What would happen if he got killed one night, and I had to stay locked in until I starved to death? I used to pace up and down, or feel my way round and round the walls inside, nearly going crazy some nights at the feeling of helplessness, of being left completely alone. I didn't know it then, of course, but I do now: it was just like being banged up in a cell.

During the daytime I went on working and scrounging. I still hadn't turned seriously to crime apart from occasionally ripping a few lead pipes out of a bombed building and selling them for scrap to make a few bob.

For relaxation—which sometimes took up most of the day
—Pancho and I used to go to one of the billiards-halls in
Stepney, where all the local young tearaways congregated.
Their leader was a long thin drink of water called Broadley.
One day I got in an argument with him and started laying
about with a cue again. He and his mates, about five of them,
waited outside for us and when we came out they jumped us.
We were outnumbered and down we went. Then someone
put the boot in and I got caught right between the eyes.
When I came round I was lying on the pavement and I
couldn't see a thing. Pancho got me up and took me off to
hospital, where I had to stay a few days until my sight came
back.

When I got out there was only one thing had to be done.
Pancho and I went to some bombed houses where they had
short iron railings in front with spikes on, fixed ourselves up
with one each, and went to look for Broadley and his mob.
We found them in somebody's basement flat, but didn't
announce ourselves, just hung around waiting. When they did
come out it was dark. I was particularly keen on doing up
Broadley himself, but in circumstances like that you don't have
time to ask someone his name before whacking him. I laid my
spike on the chap coming up the steps who I thought looked
like Broadley, and gave him a jab with it as well, as he fell.
The rest of them were so scared they retreated back in the
house again, so Pancho and I walked off.

The next day we heard it wasn't Broadley I'd done, but a
bloke called Reece, and he was dead. We knew there'd be
plenty of bother for us, so Pancho moved into the shelter with
me for a few days. Then we heard the bloke wasn't dead after
all, only fifteen stitches and concussion.

Nothing happened and nobody came looking for us, so
after a while we moved out of the shelter and went to live with
some of Pancho's friends. Soon after, I was walking down

Cable Street one day when I ran into someone I knew—a middle-aged geezer with a red face, who'd always taken a great interest in me. He was most concerned about where I'd been, how I was getting on, how glad he was to see me again, all that crap. While he was telling me he kept one hand on my arm and the other on my collar: big hands they were, sticking out of the sleeves of his blue uniform.

This cozzpot took me to the police station and in due course I was up in front of old man Henriques again. This time I thought I'd really be for it.

The bloke who ran the hostel gave evidence that I'd run away after only two days there, and how after I'd gone they'd discovered in my locker a couple of books of a near-pornographic nature called *Baby, Kiss Me Deadly* and *Lady, Don't Turn Over*. Either they'd got the wrong locker or somebody had dumped them there, because they weren't mine. I didn't read near-pornography at that age. Real pornography, yes, but the near-stuff didn't interest me any more.

Henriques said he wasn't greatly interested in my reading matter, but would somebody tell him why I'd run away? Various suggestions were offered, like me being aggressive and irresponsible, or just plain wicked. Being the man he was, he asked me as well, and when I said because I didn't like it he nodded his head as though that was what he'd thought all along.

He sent me to a remand home. The place was actually a classification centre, where they keep you for a short period to assess your potentialities, and work out the best way of dealing with you. From the way I carried on there, I should imagine they came to the conclusion the best thing in my case would be to have me shot.

I didn't know the stay would only be a short one, and I didn't know what the place was for, because naturally nobody tells you things like that. They just say: 'Don't you worry.'

So it wasn't really my fault I soon got the idea I'd been sent there to be frightened, and reacted as usual.

Everyone was put into one or other of two houses called 'Port' and 'Starboard'. Don't ask me why it had this nautical nomenclature, unless it was to match up with the general air of homosexuality. Everything was on a competitive basis between houses, and whatever you did wrong lost marks for your house.

I can't say this idea appealed to me, or even concerned me, because I couldn't see why you should suddenly be expected to show loyalty to a 'house' you'd never heard of and didn't want to belong to. So I paid no attention and went my own way, losing marks for 'Starboard' every time I took a step or opened my mouth. At the end of the week they read out the total marks of each house, and of course 'Starboard' was well down. Then they read out their rule, which was that whichever house lost all those in it didn't get their bun and cocoa on Saturday night. They also gave out the name of the boy who individually had lost the most marks for his house and went on: 'We leave it to you to deal with him as you think fit.' It was a bit like Kafka's *The Trial*—first of all no one tells you you're going to be tried, then they tell you you're guilty and in dead trouble.

Two of the leading hard cases in 'Starboard', a big bastard called Chopper Montague and a Gibraltan called Humbertz, took it on themselves as self-elected leaders of the house to give me a going-over in the dining-hall when they got me alone. All the tables had been pushed up to one end with the chairs stacked on top, and I jumped up there as soon as they started. I had to break a chair over Montague before he retired, but Humbertz was a stayer, and in the end he gave me quite a beating. From then on everyone took a punch at me whenever they got the chance, including the masters. I began to show signs of maladjustment and withdrawal, to use their terminology; black bruises and apprehension to use mine.

59

After a few days of this we were sent out on the field one day to play cricket. Half-way through one of the masters sent me back to get some more pads. I wonder if he's still out there on the pitch waiting for me to come back?

The minute I was out of his sight I got up on the boiler-house roof and hopped over the wall. I was wearing only a singlet and shorts, so when I got to the main road I started jogging along the edge of the pavement like someone training for cross-country running. After a bit I jumped on a passing bus, but the conductor found out I'd no fare money and I had to get off again. I went on like this for the whole afternoon, alternately riding and running, all the way back to Stepney. I was doing a steady two-and-a-half miles an hour up the final lap in Cable Street when I ran smack into my old pal in the blue uniform. He stood with his arms outstretched like a finishing-tape, and I was so knackered I just collapsed straight into them.

So it was back to the remand home again, the punch-ups and the no-buns-and-cocoa, and another bad week for Starboard House. Eventually, with me still not knowing what it was all about, they put me up in front of Basil Henriques again.

A probation officer told him a piece about me, in which he said my only interest seemed to be how to get out of the remand home or, failing that, how to wreck it. But he added that one day when I'd been in his office I had shown a faint interest in some model sailing ships there.

Henriques muttered something to the geezers who ran the court, and I was taken out to wait until he'd finished dealing with everyone else. Then he had me back again and took me into his office with the probation officer for a chat. Had I ever thought of the idea of going into the Merchant Navy? he asked. I hadn't, but the way he talked about it, it sounded all right, and it was certainly true I was interested in ships.

There was something about Henriques, I must say—the

way he sort of gritted his jaw and kept his voice dead calm
when he asked me if I'd go and stay at another hostel until
arrangements for me to go to sea could be made. I said yes I
would. He said: 'Very well,' with a sort of strangled sigh, and
a look in his eye like he was trying to hold up Tower Bridge
with nothing to stand on underneath. That was the last time
I ever saw him, but I've always admired him. He never lost
his temper, never panicked, had lots of patience, and always
kept calm. He would have made a good screwsman.

Off I went once more to another hostel. It wasn't Henriques'
fault it turned out to be what it was: he just had to take the
probation officer's word for it that it would suit me better than
the previous one. But in fact this one was nothing better than a
flop-house—and a religious flop-house at that—run by the
Church Army for down-and-outs. I was put in with about
sixty old men, all hawking and spitting and spewing up their
guts every night in bed, and during the day I worked in the
bakehouse, stoking up the ovens and scrubbing out tins.

I was there for several weeks, getting more and more
browned off as nothing seemed to be happening about going
to sea—and, of course, nobody told me how long it was going
on. I smoked, which was forbidden; and effed and blinded
like normal, which gave all the staff the dead needle. There
was another young boy who worked in the bakery, but lived
out, called Tommy Fossett, and we kept up a running fight
more or less every day. He was the dirtiest fighter I've ever met:
by which I mean he was dirtier than I was, and therefore
usually won. When it came to the day I was chasing him
round the bakehouse trying to clout him with a boiler-rake,
they called down one of God's right-hand men from head-
quarters to talk to me.

He told me I was a lost soul, a damned soul, and I ought to
go on my knees and pray for salvation to the Almighty. I
said I didn't believe there was a God, and if there was He

must be a stupid bastard who couldn't make things go right. His lieutenant nearly went potty, screaming and raving, calling me a foul-mouthed heretic and a wicked, perverted monster. He got so worked up he grabbed me round the throat and shook me, so I hooked him one in the guts and walked out. Tommy Fossett decided to come with me: after all, he and I had more in common, and more respect for each other, than either of us had for the Holy Joes.

He knew some people in Wimbledon, so he took me over there and introduced me to two of his mates who put us up in their flat. They were both making a steady living at drumming. Nothing sensational, but failing the Merchant Navy it seemed as good a way of making a living as any, so we all teamed up, got ourselves organized with a car, and began knocking off houses in Surrey.

We were quite unselective, screwing unoccupied houses one after the other, three or four a day. It was amateurish and senseless, an uneducated way of thieving, but it's a stage a lot of young criminals go through, like an apprenticeship. Try a suitable-looking house, knock on the front door; if there's no reply, round the back, in through a window, fill your pockets with small stuff, out—and on to the next.

I was never scared, even at the beginning; just busy going through drawers, dressing-tables, cupboards, vases, and any other hiding places. Mostly we took ready cash. Lumbering yourself up with clothing is hard work, and jewellery is bad value for kids, because you can easily get took on by a fence who'll tell you it's imitation.

It was surprising how many people did leave cash lying around. In one house, which belonged to a high-ranking army officer, there was over £800 scattered about in drawers and vases, and, for some reason I've never fathomed, it was all in dirty ten-shilling notes.

In this fashion the four of us made quite a good living. We

dressed well, ate well, went to dog racing and cinemas, got ourselves birds whenever we fancied them, and generally had a good time for ourselves. After all, the war was on, so we weren't the only people living dangerously. In a pub one night a Yank offered me a shooter for £10 and I bought it off him. I never used it, but could easily have done if the opportunity had arisen. When it did I hadn't got it with me.

Fossett and I were picked up by a couple of cozzpots in an air-raid shelter in Bayswater where we'd gone for a quiet night during the bombing. I had a duffed-up identity card, and we were taken to the police station for questioning. Being stupid, when they asked my address I gave the first I could think of, which was the religious flop-house. Naturally, when the police phoned there, they were told I hadn't been seen for some considerable time. They put Fossett in one cell and me in another, and after a few hours a detective came down and gave me what passes in the Metropolitan Police for clever stuff. The hoary old one: 'Your mate's spilled his guts and given us a statement admitting all you've done. If you tell us all you know, you can get your own back by putting him in trouble as well.'

I told him where to put it. But the terrible thing was Fossett really had told them, and we were both slung in Wormwood Scrubs on remand, charged with a long list of housebreakings.

There was no Henriques in the Juvenile Court this time: just three right unsympathetic bastards of magistrates, with whom nothing cut any ice.

A probation officer said a piece about the hopes for me going in the Merchant Navy and the wife of the army officer whose house we'd done spoke up too. She said she'd like me to have a chance to redeem myself, and hoped they'd let me go to sea—which I thought was very fine, considering what they'd lost. But the magistrates wouldn't have it. I can't say I blame them. The chairman said the Merchant Navy was a fine service with wonderful traditions, and he didn't want to risk spoiling it by putting me into it. A right unsympathetic bastard, like I said. He ordered me to approved school, and the one chosen was Carlton, Bedfordshire.

I had to be taken up there by a plain-clothes screw who wasn't going to run risks, and he put handcuffs on me as soon as he collected me at the Scrubs. I said I wasn't going like that and he'd have to carry me every step of the way: I sat down on the floor. We argued the toss, until finally he said he'd take them off as soon as we were on the train at St Pancras, so off we went with a raincoat between us to cover up the cuffs.

When we got on to St Pancras I said: 'All right, what about your promise?'

What he'd actually promised was when we got on the train, but when I made as if I was going to sit down right there on the station concourse he weakened. As he was turning the key in the cuffs he said: 'Now you won't try anything silly, boy, will you?' I hadn't time to answer because I was away through the booking-hall.

Just my luck, two coppers were walking up the approach, and something made them suspicious—either me running like a streak, perhaps, or the shouting and screaming of the screw as he chased after me. Anyway, one of them stuck out his foot and down I went with all three of them on top of me until my keeper got the cuffs back on again. He acted all hurt and sensitive about it, and we stayed cuffed-up for the rest of the journey. Some people are very untrusting.

There's been a lot in the news recently about Carlton School—the inquiry, talk of boys getting bashed about and caned, and so on. Of course in the days when I was there things were different: for one, there was no inquiry.

The headmaster was a bloke called Charles Wathen, an

optimist if ever I met one. 'You'll like it here,' he said, when I was up for interview on arrival. 'Don't look on it as anything other than an ordinary school, because that's what it is. Forget about it being a place you've been sent to as punishment.'

He really believed this himself. He was tremendously proud of the school and the achievements of his pupils, and he was always telling us we were as good as every other boy in any school.

The first thing I did when I got there was leave, but, as the place was right out in the middle of nowhere in the country, I didn't get far before I was caught. Wathen had me up in front of him. He didn't get angry, just pointed out I was silly and would have to be moved to a Borstal if I didn't behave, and they were dreadful places which I wouldn't be happy at. He gave me a few swishes with his cane, nothing serious, and left it at that: he didn't hold it against me, neither then nor any other time when I did anything wrong.

Because I discovered that all the real villains were in the joinery class, I said that was the trade I wanted to learn. When I got into it, I discovered two very surprising things. One was I could actually do joinery; and the other that I liked doing it. The master was an outright fanatic: he wanted two pieces of wood joined together like an engineer marries metal, and he had the gift of getting you just as keen as he was to do it absolutely perfectly.

A month or two after I started at Carlton the war in Europe finished. On V.E. Day I had it away to London with another boy: we wandered around Trafalgar Square and the other places where the crowds were, but all we had between us was seven-and-sixpence, so we didn't have much to celebrate on. Late at night we walked into a police station and gave ourselves up. When we got back to Carlton, Wathen gave us a talking-to which neither he nor us took very seriously, and a couple of perfunctory swishes. That was all, and once again it was forgotten the next day.

Since I'd run away twice, I can't have been very high on the list of good security risks. But not long afterwards Wathen called me up and told me one of my younger brothers was living in a children's home in Bedford. Would I like to go and see him? When I said I would, all he asked me was to give him my word I'd come back, and he gave me money out of his own pocket for the bus fare.

I spent a couple of hours at the home with my brother. The bus was late coming back, and I got in a good hour after the time I should have done. Two of the staff had already collected on bets they'd made that I wouldn't return, and I got a nasty kick out of knowing they had to give it back and pay out on top.

From then on I went out to see my brother regularly. I haven't been trusted a lot in my time, and I was under a big obligation to Wathen, because he would really have been in trouble if I'd absconded. Even if I'd gone some other time, not on one of the visits to my brother, it would have looked as if I'd made arrangements for it while I was out on his parole.

Once I saw my father. He came from up north where he was working, to stay in a nearby town with some relatives. Wathen gave me permission to join him for two days. My father had been writing regularly to me at Carlton, and I could tell when we met he still cared a lot about what became of me, although he'd more or less given up hope of having any influence on me himself. I remember him asking me if I behaved myself. 'Oh sure,' I said. 'You know. . . .'

He nodded. 'Sure, I know . . . and if they've got another three hundred like you, God help the poor bastards.'

I wasn't all that far from being happy at Carlton. I enjoyed the joinery, and I read a lot. Their own library wasn't up to much, but I arranged with other boys to bring me back books from the public library in the town, so I didn't do so badly. It was there I first came across Oscar Wilde—*The Ballad of Reading Gaol*, naturally—but that led me on to his other works, and I still rate him the tops. I went through most of Dickens, and a lot of Somerset Maugham. *Cakes and Ale* I didn't take to, but *Liza of Lambeth* and *Alien Corn* were terrific, particularly *Liza* which I've reread several times since.

I discovered Upton Sinclair, Theodore Dreiser, Scott Fitzgerald, George Orwell. *Seven Pillars of Wisdom* I thought a fantastically good book, but the other Lawrence, D. H., never appealed: I thought he was a creep. I liked some of Hemingway, but when I found out he enjoyed bull-fighting I went off him.

One time I gave myself about fifteen headaches trying to get through James Joyce's *Ulysses*, but I just wasn't up to it intellectually, although I'm always kidding myself that some day I'm going to try again. I liked a few poets too: Auden, Robert Graves, William Plomer, and, of course, Dylan Thomas. But I can't 'get' poetry unless I read it aloud, and I'm too embarrassed to do this in front of anyone else. I even liked Kipling, but only for the jingle, not the jingoism.

Well, as I say, I wasn't exactly miserable at Carlton with the way things were going. Wathen wanted me and another boy to take the City and Guilds examinations, and after a lot of effort he got us both accepted for further training at a technical college. I think he was himself very pleased at achieving this—and I know I was. It meant I was going to be properly trained for something I enjoyed: it meant I was going to have a trade and a skill that would last me all my life. I got really excited about it.

Then I got my call-up papers for the Army.

They passed me A1 at the medical and asked me what I wanted to go in. I said: 'Nothing,' but they wouldn't have that, naturally. So that put paid to the technical college.

When I went to say goodbye to Wathen he gave me a couple of quid on top of what I was officially supposed to have, again out of his own pocket, and said he hoped I'd write to him if I was in trouble, or even if I wasn't. After I'd gone in the Army he wrote me four times, always in his own handwriting. The last one said: *I shan't be writing again after this if you don't reply, because I don't want you to feel you're under an obligation to write back.*

I still didn't reply, and that was the last I heard: but I know if we ever met again he wouldn't hold it against me.

To say I wasn't a big success in the Army wouldn't be true: I wasn't any kind of success at all. Over things like regulations and discipline, our points of view were diametrically opposite. The Army's all right for wooden-heads who like playing soldiers—but for wooden-heads who don't, like me, it's a waste of time; particularly theirs.

For six weeks I was in training barracks at Bury St Edmunds. On the second day I found out that if you were too stupid to understand simple orders, like 'Halt' and 'Right wheel', they took you out of the squad and told you to stand at the side, watching others to see how it should be done. If that was how they defined stupid, it was O.K. by me, and I left the marching up and down to the really intelligent ones.

We had several other misunderstandings too, like when I blancoed my webbing greener than Killarney when everyone else had theirs a smart Mersey-mud colour, and got taken out of the parade as a punishment. Another time I had a ruck with the Padre in a discussion group by telling him I thought he was a hypocrite because people oughtn't to be pious about killing others. I'm not exactly a thirty-second commercial for Christianity myself, of course, but at least if I was going in for murder I wouldn't look up texts in the Bible to excuse myself. Perhaps that's why Monty got on in the Army and I didn't.

After what they called 'training' was over, I put down to go in an Airborne regiment and was sent up to Chesterfield. The third night I was there I got mixed up in a fight in the market place with another soldier. He was an Irish bastard, but really game. I gave him a terrific belting all round the stalls until he sagged against a wall, wearily shaking his head and asking me if I'd finished. When I said: 'Yes,' he said: 'Right then, now I'll start'—and proceeded to give me a terrible shellacking in return, knocking me all the way back round the market the way we'd come. He'd half killed me by the time the Redcaps turned up and pulled us both in.

You're not supposed to fight in the Army, at least not against your own side, so I was sent back to my unit as unsuitable for Airborne. I loafed around for a while at barracks, then was accepted into a Combined Ops outfit for training as a commando. The next three months I really enjoyed: scrambling up and down cliffs, swinging across streams on ropes, crawling across ground under Bren-gun fire, unarmed combat, and learning how to creep up behind sentries and knife them. There was discipline, but not much, and I felt there was some point to the whole business. But then Combined Ops was disbanded, and back I went to my original unit, from where I was put in the Service Corps.

It was terrible, all bullshit and monotony, and after a while I went absent. After a few days in Norwich the Redcaps nicked me, and I ended up in Colchester glasshouse, doing a spell of refined army punishment, like running on the spot, in the full heat of August, in full service marching order: buttoned-up overcoats, helmets, packs, rifles, the lot. I don't know what this is supposed to do for you except fill you with black hatred for the bastards who put you through it.

69

I got in more trouble as soon as I was back with the unit. They were sent to Germany, and reluctantly I had to go too. 'Reluctantly' about describes it: I was in handcuffs, which weren't taken off until we arrived at Hamburg.

We sloshed around for a while, showing the Germans how superior we were to them by fighting among ourselves, bartering bars of chocolate or soap for girls, drinking, and plundering anything we could lay hands on. In their own way, victors are even less dignified than the defeated, and always have been through history.

I was trudging down a street one day in a small town, fed up with the sour joke called the Army, and went into a dingy restaurant for a cup of *ersatz* coffee. At another table I saw three people: the man a cartoonist's dream of a Prussian, fat, bull-necked, with a square head and cropped hair, a real stone Bismarck; his wife, very severe and drab, sharp-featured, all arsenic and no lace; and a girl. Unlike every other German female I'd seen up till then, she had none of the marks of defeat and privation. She looked fresh, young, healthy, lively; and after a while, noticing my staring, she gave a little smile, which disappeared quick when she saw her mother looking at her.

When they went out I followed, and saw them go into the post office across the street. I went in after them, and started filling up a form on the writing-table, pretending I wasn't there. The girl was idly scribbling on a blotter while she waited for her parents to finish at the counter. When they'd gone out I walked over to see what she'd written. It was *Rathaus. 19.00.*

At seven o'clock that evening I was outside the Town Hall waiting. She was nervous and dithering when she turned up, telling me her parents had always told her she wasn't to speak to soldiers, so we went and had a cup of coffee while I told her how right they were. Her English, which she'd learned at school, was very good, and one way and another we built up quite an understanding. Her name was Lisa.

It was obvious that as far as sex was concerned I wasn't going to get any, and this really intrigued me because, as I've said, every other German girl I'd met would let you have her for five cigarettes or a bar of chocolate. We met often, sometimes for a walk, sometimes for a few cups of coffee.

The weeks went by. I was still drawing a blank as far as anything physical was concerned, and I was getting really stuck on her. Then one night she said she was going to Luneberg in a few days, to stay with her aunt for a fortnight, and she hoped I'd find a way of getting over to see her. The next day in camp there was a call for volunteers for guard duty at, of all places, Luneberg: and for the first time ever I actually volunteered for something in the Army. I thought the sergeant-major had said it was for D.P. duty—displaced persons—but what he'd really said was D.B.—detention barracks. This I didn't discover until I was put in charge of some poor mug I had to take up to Luneberg in handcuffs. The last time I'd had them on somebody had been taking me, which just goes to show what can happen in the Army.

They'd taken the precaution of not giving me a key for the cuffs, so, although we both worked like hell on them all the time we were on the train, they were still on when the reception party met us at the station. I was pushed straight back on the train as soon as I'd handed him over, and never even got out of the station at Luneberg.

But only a few days later there was yet another call for volunteers for Luneberg, and it really was for D.P. guards. Once more I stepped up. This time the destination was changed at the last minute and I went off to Oldenburg instead, as a guard on a train carrying about two hundred displaced persons who were going to be put in a disused army camp.

71

We were issued with ammunition, and given orders to shoot anyone who tried to jump off the train. Fortunately none of them did, or at least I didn't see any. Doing that job, I've never felt more degraded in all my life. These were free people, in this position because they were the remnants of Germany's slave-labour force, who'd been taken from their homes thousands of miles away. And now here we were, shoving them into old trains like cattle, and dumping them in nameless camps. Their only possessions were palliasse-cases filled with straw and a few odd scraps of clothing. They hadn't asked to be there, and they didn't want to be there. After all they'd suffered from the Germans, now they were still being pushed about as though they weren't real living human beings but just bloody nuisances. The only crime they'd committed was being alive.

Being a regular fiddler, I had plenty of chocolates and cigarettes to hand out. Old men, old women, and a lot who looked old but weren't, all of them thin and starving, many of them diseased and dying—they stretched out their hands gratefully and took what I offered, the women ready quite automatically to give their bodies in return. It was all they'd got to give and they'd done it often before.

I got no women for my chocolate, nor anything else either —no pleasure from giving, no feeling of being generous, nothing: only shame at being in my position while those poor bastards were in theirs.

When we reached our destination, and the guard duty was done, I went absent again. There were about ten times the number of deserters in Germany as the official figures admit, and it wasn't difficult to get by. Naafi canteens were dead easy to knock off: one good kick was usually enough to break in the door, there were plenty of cigarettes and chocolate inside, and these were easily bartered for food and drink. I also picked up a couple of pay books and a book of leave passes, so I was well set up and lived well for several weeks before the Redcaps got me.

There was another fifty-six days in the glasshouse, and then I was transferred to a tank-transporter unit near Hamburg. A few days later in the town I ran into Lisa again.

I'd never really got her out of my mind despite the few dozen one-night stands I'd had in between, and it was pretty obvious too that she was still stuck on me. If I wasn't in love with her, at least I wasn't far off getting to be. We took up where we'd left off. There was still no sex. But it was funny, it still didn't put me off.

One night we were in a café having a cup of coffee and talking, when some other soldiers came in and started having a go at us. She was very pretty, and they were all making guesses how many bars of chocolate I'd bought her for. This was giving me the needle, and when one of them came over to her with a grin on his big, stupid mug, holding out some cigarettes and saying: 'How about these for a quick one?' I went wild. I kicked over the table at him and jumped in with both boots in his guts. His mates came to the rescue and soon the whole place was rocking, with chairs and tables flying, and beer bottles appearing in people's hands as well. Lisa started screaming and crying, and I grabbed hold of her arm and dragged her out, picking up a broken bottle on the way and ramming it into the face of anyone who tried to stop us.

So Lisa at last saw me as I really was: and it shocked her sick. My thin veneer of civilization had slipped and she saw what was underneath: viciousness, savagery, brutality. For hours afterwards she couldn't look me in the face, and we just walked around without saying a word. She never said anything about it, either that night or later, as though she didn't want to believe it had happened. Women are funny: because that night, later, in a park, she let me have her.

From then on it was regular, until the day we found I'd

put her up the spout and she got in a terrific panic about what her parents would say and do to her. We decided we'd go away together, and she slipped home while her parents were out, packed her case, and came to meet me at Hamburg station.

I left her on the platform while I went to get tickets. I was in civilian clothes, and there was a crush at the ticket office. A German copper started pushing everyone around; I pushed him back, and before I knew what time it was he'd whistled up two of his mates and they swagged me off to their police station.

It was more than my life was worth to let on I was British, because they'd have handed me over to the Redcaps right away, so I went dumb. They stuck me in the flowery and brought along all sorts of people to try and talk to me. Poles, Latvians, French, American, British, Swedes, God knows what. After three days I was still dumb. Then one morning I dropped a bowl of hot soup on my foot, and, of course, I started effing and blinding. Even Germans recognize pure English when they hear it, so that was that. Back to the glasshouse for fifty-six days once more.

Lisa meantime had waited and wondered and worried because I didn't come back with the tickets, and must have thought I'd run out on her. What happened I've never found out, although I did hear later she'd miscarried, which was perhaps as well, all things considered. It took me a hell of a time to forget about her, but there's no doubt she was well shut of me in the end.

After the reformative influence of the glasshouse, I was sent back once more to my unit, who by now were getting almost as sick of me as I was of them. I started to do quite a bit of drinking, which I hadn't gone in for much before, and staggered back to camp night after night in what was called 'an unsoldierly fashion', i.e. sloshed.

I was lurching through the gate one night when an officer came out, and pulled me up for not saluting. I was pretty drunk and took a swing at him, so he called out the guardroom squad, who bundled me into a cell. A regimental police corporal came in to question me, and I clouted him as soon as he opened the door, so they banged it shut again quick.

After about half an hour the orderly sergeant arrived. I heard him say outside: 'All right, open it up and we'll see how tough he really is.' I didn't care for the sound of it. The only thing handy was a long wooden form in the cell, so I took up a position at the far end of the cell, holding it like a battering-ram. When the door opened I charged. The form hit him straight in the chest, knocking him backwards out of the door: his boots shot from under him on the stone floor, and there was a terrible crack when his head hit ground. I slung the form out after him, and then about five assorted corporals and sergeants appeared in a rush. I thought they were after me, but they weren't: all they were bothered with was getting the door shut.

They left me alone for nearly the whole of the following day, giving me plenty of time to sober up and reflect what trouble I was in. The very least I could think of that would happen was I'd be shot. Late in the afternoon one of the corporals shouted through the door: 'They've sent for Captain Randell to deal with you.' This did nothing to cheer me up at all, because I'd heard of Randell. He had the reputation of knowing everything there is about all-in fighting, and was rumoured to eat two tough soldiers every day for breakfast.

He arrived the next day. He banged on the door, and said in a voice that sounded as though it ran on tank-tracks: 'This is Captain Randell and I'm coming in. If you want trouble, lad, you can have it. Stand away from the door.'

He looked as though he weighed about fifteen stone, and he had long hair almost down to his collar. This didn't mean he was in any way delicate. I naturally expected him to give me a working-over first, to be on the safe side: but instead he just sat down on the edge of the bed and said: 'Shall we have a talk?'

That's what we did. We both knew I was in dead trouble, but he was quite sympathetic, saying he felt some of the people I'd whacked probably deserved it. Unfortunately, the orderly sergeant was in hospital with a fractured skull. Randell said arrangements had been made for me to be examined at a hospital, if I would agree, and he hoped I'd co-operate as it might prove in my best interests in the end. As he was a reasonable sort of character, I said I would.

Two days later they took me out in handcuffs to this hospital. Randell hadn't said what sort it was: it turned out to be a nut-house. They gave me all the tests they could think of, and whatever the result it still didn't make me unfit for the Army, or not responsible for my actions, which I could have told them myself anyway.

I was given a court martial. Randell had agreed to defend me when I asked him, although he wasn't a qualified brief, and he did his best to find something good to say about me without departing too far from the truth. The president of the court wasn't impressed. 'You're no asset to the British Army,' he said, 'only a liability. Where do you hope to get by this sort of behaviour?'

'Out,' I said, pugnaciously. At least it was honest, even if it wasn't very clever.

'Well, you won't,' said the president, going red. 'Because I'm giving you three years' imprisonment instead.'

For some reason known only to Command, the sentence was reduced by half on confirmation. I hoped I might be sent back to England to do it, but I wasn't.

3

The Criminal Does Not Change

W<small>HEN</small> I came out of prison the time for my discharge had
gone by, and at least I was out of the Army. We parted from
each other with mutual contempt. I'd half a mind to stay in
Germany because there was a good living to be made with
all the rackets going on. But the people who'd been home told
me things were really rocking in London with all the shortages
and black-market demand. I decided to go back and get in
on it.

Going straight? I never even gave it a thought.

Right away in London I got into business, chiefly on
buying and selling petrol and clothing coupons. It was easy,
and the only thing wrong was I had to depend on other people
for supplies, which were erratic and unsatisfactory: not business-
like, in fact. So I started getting my own, breaking into offices,
shops, garages, with a bit of ordinary screwing on the side.

Large blocks of flats in areas where wealthy people lived,
like Knightsbridge and Chelsea for instance, paid very well.
I rather fancied myself as a bit of an acrobat, and used to
work from a rope fastened up on the roof, letting myself down
outside until I came to a suitable window. There were always
plenty of watches and jewellery lying about, and I soon learned
how to value them before offering to a fence.

One evening I was in a flat when the woman who lived there came home. She started screaming for help, so I had to belt her. I'm not keen on using violence on women, but there's no choice if they start making a row.

It dawned on me after a bit that instead of picking up odds and ends it'd be quicker and more profitable to start further back along the line. I got up a firm with one or two reliable thieves, and we went into what might be called the wholesale side, knocking off any marketable commodity: cigarettes, groceries, cloth; on one occasion, just before Christmas, we had a vanload of nuts that fetched quite a respectable price.

I was learning all the time. Always find a buyer before doing a job, for instance. That way you don't get left holding stuff, and have to let it go cheap to get rid of it. Also that fences' houses are good places to screw; they can't very well scream about losing something they know is stolen.

Work was steady, living was comfortable, and I got myself a flat near Victoria and a car. My income level was on average well over a hundred a week, and on that standard you can have as many birds as you like, when you like.

But all good things come to an end. One Easter Sunday morning I was captured on the roof of some flats in Highgate, and taken up to the Sessions in front of Fulton who was known as the 'Pontoon King'. He lived up to his reputation and I got twenty-one months, which I did in the Scrubs. It was dead easy compared with the army prison.

When I came out my old friend Pancho was at the gate to meet me. He took me over to Croydon where some friends of his called Ken and Paul lived. They looked after me because I was a friend of his, seeing I was all right for clothing and money as required.

They were working themselves at the wage-snatch business, with a bit of smash-and-grab on the side, and took me into their firm. We got on steadily for several months without any trouble. The living was much more reliable than screwing, where you were taking a chance on what you were going to get.

Smash-and-grab can only be done properly as a team job, and so long as everyone knows what he's doing, and does it, it's fairly easy. You need a car, and a hook on a chain fastened to the back, to pull away the window-grille. The car backs up, you slam the hook through the grille into the glass, the car pulls the grille away, and you thrash in what's left of the window with an iron bar, taking care to knock out any jagged pieces sticking up from the bottom, otherwise you can cut your arms reaching over it. At the same time your other men are moving in a couple of paces behind you to start hauling the stuff out.

I always carry two bars; one to thrash the window with, and a smaller one to use on anyone who tries to interfere. Once in a while I had to put it about, but usually we were away before trouble arrived.

One night we were doing a West End jeweller's, and the police whizzed round the corner the moment the hook went through the glass. Somebody'd tipped them, probably a bird Paul had had a ruck with the night before and slung out. There was a bit of a punch-up, but they were ready for that, too. Pancho wasn't with us, so he was all right: but Paul and Ken got three years each, and I got two.

I did it in Wandsworth, and lost a bit of remission for fighting. When I came out Pancho got me in with another smash-and-grab outfit who took me on a job the very first night in Hendon. It paid well, and my whack was more than enough to live on for several months if I'd wanted to.

But I've always been what you might call a journeyman thief. I believe in working steadily, not just when you need money. That way you take risks and do things because necessity is driving you. I did a few more wage-snatches with this firm, and I got interested, too, in safe-breaking, going out a few times with experts to learn how it was done until I could branch out on my own.

There are three main ways, depending on the circumstances you've got to work under. The quickest is blowing. You pack gelignite into the lock with a knitting-needle, push in detonator and wires, and cover the whole lot with plasticene. Then you pile rugs, carpets, coats, or anything else like that round to deaden the noise, and run the wires out of the door, round a corner, somewhere safe. A small battery will give you all the charge you need to set it off.

Another way is with the acetylene blower. For this you've got to build yourself a collapsible tent first, out of wooden struts and canvas, and you work behind it so the light won't show. When you've plenty of time, this is a good method.

A third, and the one I, personally, like best, is to get at the back of the safe, if you can, and work out one of the rivets with a hammer and cold-chisel. Once you've got one out, all you need do then is put your cane in at the edge, and lever. The other rivets shoot out one after the other just like bullets.

Time went on until I was captured again, this time out on the Watford by-pass driving a lorryload of copper we'd knocked off. The motor was poor and the load was heavy, so the police car passed me easily. I got two years for that, and did it in Pentonville. Pancho was doing bird there himself at the same time for something else, and we came out more or less together, setting up again with two other friends straight away. Again it was mostly wage-snatches and safes.

I got took in after a few months on a G.B.H. (Grievous Bodily Harm). I tuned up a bloke in a club with a starting-handle. It was a personal matter which had nothing to do with the Law, but they tried to make a case of it because they knew

I'd been getting away with other things they hadn't caught me for.

As the bloke who'd been hurt was only another thief, the Law weren't making a dead set at a conviction. But they hung on to me until I made their bung big enough. In the end it cost me five hundred quid before they'd say in court they weren't sure they'd got the right man, and the case was dismissed. I'd probably have got five years, so it was just about worth it.

Then I was captured trying to break a safe in a private house at Richmond. The judge I was put up in front of decided for some reason I was ripe for Corrective Training, and gave me three years which I did in Nottingham and Liverpool.

When I came out I had to report once a month to a probation officer. He was quite a decent bloke, and we agreed I'd give going straight a try. During C.T. I'd learned painting and decorating, so I started a job with a firm of contractors who did mostly school and hospital work. It was so dull it nearly drove me potty, sloshing green paint on miles of wall for weeks on end, and after three weeks I packed it in.

I went on seeing the probation officer, and was supposed to be looking for another job. He could probably have guessed from my prosperous appearance that I was working all right, but not at the sort of thing I was meant to be. Still, there wasn't much he could do about it, and he didn't really try, knowing it would make no difference.

Somebody grassed me for one job: an office-breaking in the City, where I was after the safe. An insurance man had given a friend the tip there was supposed to be about £70,000 in it. Naturally the friend didn't touch it himself, but passed it on to me on a share basis. I'd only just got in the place when the Law turned up, and I had to dive out pretty quick, so they missed me and nothing came of it. For me, that is. But I found out who'd done the grassing, and gave him a stripe one night

F

when he was stood at a street-corner kissing his girl. So then the grass had an even wider mouth than before. I don't use a razor for striping. A lino-knife's better.

Then I got three years for pussy-hoisting from a warehouse in the City. The police car following my van had to touch seventy along the Mile End Road before they got past. I rammed them but it didn't put them off. They all piled out and grabbed me. It was a bit fierce while it lasted, but there were four of them. I got the worst of it. I was given three years, which was reasonable.

Pancho was inside when I came out, but Paul and Ken were around. We teamed up. Things went all right for a bit. I worked at whatever came along. Then there was a big balls-up over a job at Harlesden; I was clobbered by a bank guard. I got four years. It could have been more.

Pancho met me at the gate when I came out. He took me to some friends. They looked after me. They took me in on a job at Hendon. It was a wages-snatch.

2

An Honest Man?

*Up to this point, Bob, we've concentrated on what
might be called the narrative of your life, trying to
trace your development into the person you now are.*

*Now I want to discuss with you some of the points
that arise from that, and elaborate on your attitudes
and ideas. . . .*

My first question is this: If you were to describe yourself in one word, would the description invariably be 'A criminal'?

Yes, definitely. That's what I am, I never think of myself in any other way.

And have you any intention of changing, of going straight or reforming?

None whatsoever. There's one thing, though, I'd like to make clear right at the start—and that is, I don't want to try and pass myself off as a 'master criminal' or anything like that. I'm not. I've had successes and failures in life like everyone else, and I'm nothing out of the ordinary as far as criminals go. I don't consider myself cleverer than most, or even cleverer than the police, for example: sometimes I have been, and quite obviously sometimes not. On the whole I'd say I was just the ordinary run of professional criminal, similar to—well, let's say to a bank clerk from Surbiton in the straight world. But having said that, still definitely 'a criminal', yes.

And would you say your earnings were comparable with those of a Surbiton bank clerk?

I don't know what he'd earn—quite honestly, I don't know how much I've made in my time either, because I haven't kept accounts to show to the income tax. My earnings have usually been large sums of money spread over short periods of time—both in the getting and the spending. I've gone into a club, a gambling place, not once but many times, with two or three hundred quid in my pocket—and come out with exactly nothing. One time a girl took sixty quid out of my pocket and I never even noticed it'd gone until somebody told me months afterwards she'd had it. And at other times I've had only about fourpence in the world. It's so irregular, you see, it's difficult to say just how much I have had from crime. I should say that if I worked it all out with pencil and paper, relying on my memory which is faulty at the best of times, and then dividing the whole lot by ten or twelve for the number of years I've been at it seriously . . . well, it'd come out at about £2000 or £2500 a year, perhaps a little bit more. We'd better change that first idea to a bank *manager* from Surbiton, I suppose, hadn't we? Still, the point's the same: that sort of figure, which is as near as I can get on a calculation, is not a tremendously rich living from crime or anything else, is it? Especially when you take into account how quick I spend it when I've got it. All the same, I don't know of a straight job I could do that'd bring me in that yearly income.

Is there any particular form of crime, or criminal activity, which you wouldn't commit?

A year or two ago I used to think I'd never go in for drug-trafficking, but now I'm not so sure about that. I've never actually done it yet, but as I get older I seem to be losing my inhibitions, I don't feel as strongly about it as I used to. There's only one thing I still feel I could never do, and that's poncing. To me it's the worst thing of the lot, I'd never stoop to it—or at least I hope I wouldn't. Maybe I'm old-fashioned, or sentimental about women or something—but I just can't stomach the idea of poncing at all. I've nothing but contempt, real, deep contempt, for ponces.

There's no other limit you'd set yourself?

No. I'll go as far as necessary, whatever it is.

What does that mean, exactly?

What it says. If it was ever necessary to kill somebody, well, I'd go up to and including that. I'd kill somebody in a fit of temper, I'm quite capable of that—or if they were trying to stop me getting something I'd really made up my mind to have. Or if they were holding me down, and there was so much at stake that I'd just got to get away. But I think most people have it in them to do murder at some time in their lives, under certain circumstances.

The thing which I find most difficult to understand about you is that you're apparently quite undeterred by your repeated prison sentences. You've now reached the stage, with your record, that when you're caught next time it's more than likely you'll get about eight years' preventive detention. I don't understand how you can be prepared to face that.

I'm not prepared. This is the thing which people like you can never grasp. I'm no more 'prepared' to do eight years' P.D. than you're prepared to knock somebody down in your car tomorrow. I don't think too much about the one more than you do about the other. It's an ever-present risk but one doesn't dwell on it—do you see what I mean?

I've always got this thing in my mind, and so have most other criminals like me—'it won't be this time that I'll get caught'. Prison only becomes the dominant thought when you're actually back in the prison cell—or no, to be realistic, perhaps a bit before that, when you're actually in the arms of a police officer, although even then you've still got some hope you might not end up in the nick.

Occasionally I get the vague idea that if men who'd been in prison were to go back and contemplate the prison wall from outside, just before they set out on a job, they mightn't do it. But it wouldn't work. You see, three days after you've come out of prison, however long the sentence, you've forgotten all about it. You've forgotten the caged-up feeling, the monotonous food, the smell of latrines, the piggishness of the screws, the soul-destroying torture of visiting-boxes with your friends having to shout a conversation with you through plate-glass— it's all gone, soon after you come out, and you do everything you can to make it go, too.

Then one day one of your mates comes along and says: 'I've heard of a peter wants blowing, it's got two grand in it,

87

you want to come in on it and make one?' So you knock down the amount by 50% because people exaggerate, and you think: 'Well, at least I'll have a look at it, there's no harm in that.'

So he takes you along to look at the set-up, you weigh it up and work it out, and you think: 'Well, this is an absolute doddle, it can't miss; yes, of course I'll do it.' So you say to your mate: 'O.K., sure I'll come in, when do we start?' It doesn't even occur to you that there's even a chance you might get nicked, it all looks so easy. And where's your 'prepared' gone then?

I don't want to do eight years, no—but if I have to I have to, and that's all there is to it. If you're a criminal, what's the alternative to the risk of going to prison? Coal-miners don't spend their time worrying about the risk they might get killed by a fall at the coal-face either. Prison's an occupational risk, that's all—and one I'm quite prepared to take. I'll willingly gamble away a third of my life in prison, so long as I can live the way I want for the other two-thirds. After all, it's my life, and that's how I feel about it. The alternative— the prospect of vegetating the rest of my life away in a steady job, catching the 8.13 to work in the morning, and the 5.50 back again at night, all for ten or fifteen quid a week—now that really does terrify me, far more than the thought of a few years in the nick.

You don't think, then, that there's anything wrong in not working for your living?

But I do work for my living. Most crime—unless it's the senseless, petty-thieving sort—is quite hard work, you know. Planning a job, working out all the details of the best way to do it—and then carrying it out, under a lot of nervous strain and tension—and having to run round afterwards, if it's goods, fencing the stuff, getting a good price for it, delivering it to the fence, and so on—all this needs a lot of thinking and effort

88

and concentration. It certainly is 'work', don't kid yourself about that.

But anyway this whole point's not all that simple. A lot of other people don't 'work' for their living, in the way you mean —but nobody goes on at them like they do at criminals. Quite a large proportion of the 'upper classes', for instance. You can see them any day round Piccadilly, Vigo Street, Savile Row—nattily dressed half-wits who've never done a stroke of work in their lives, popping in and out of Fortnum's or Scott's, spending all their time trying to get rid of the money their fathers and grandfathers and great-grandfathers left them. And usually it's that sort who get fiercest about people like me, saying we ought to be caned and whipped and flogged because we never do an honest day's work.

I can steal from people like that without the faintest compunction at all, in fact I'm delighted to do it. I remember once screwing the town house of the Duke of . . . well, I'd better not say who, because I didn't get caught for it. The inside of the house was the most beautiful place I've ever been in in my life—gorgeous curtains and furnishings, antique furniture, silver bowls and vases all over the place, exquisite miniatures on the walls—it was a fabulous place. My only regret was I hadn't got a furniture van so I could strip it from top to bottom. His Lordship I suppose was up in Scotland shooting wild birds, or some other civilized hobby, and his house was just standing unused until he chose to come back and live in it again.

I remember after I'd come out I passed an old man in rags, standing on the street-corner scraping at a violin to try and earn himself a few coppers, and I thought: 'You mug, why don't you go in there and at least get yourself a good sleep in one of his Lordship's unused beds for a night.'

All the things that were in that house, all those beautiful possessions, the duke had got for himself without the faintest effort of any kind. Most of them had been handed down to him, and all he'd ever had to do to get the others was write out a cheque—and he probably didn't even do that for himself but had a flunkey to do it. Never in his whole life had he known what it was like to be short of anything. Well, I had, and I don't think it was wrong to steal enough from him to subsidize me for a bit.

And those people, when they have something nicked, they've got it all insured anyway, so they don't suffer. Sometimes they advertise for its return—you know, 'Sentimental value' and all that. I'm sure I'd feel sentimental, too, about losing something worth a few hundred quid, only I'd be a bit more honest about it.

And the stuff I pinched from that particular house I appreciated, I did really. In fact, if it hadn't been too dangerous, I'd gladly have kept a lot of it to have around my own place, because it was so beautiful. But I never felt bad about taking it—why should I? I felt terrific. He'd got no cause for complaint, because it was taken, after all, by someone who could really appreciate its artistic merit, not one of those insensitive thugs who couldn't differentiate between Royal Worcester and a Woolworth's chamber-pot.

Oh yes, and one more thing. A couple of years later I read in the papers how this particular duke was involved in a real sordid court case. The details that came out about his private life then made me wonder if he ever did really appreciate those lovely possessions he had. From what they dragged out he sounded a right stinking bastard. But if I'd been caught that time I screwed his place he'd have been all up in arms about me—and the Law would have taken his side too. He was respectable and I wasn't, that's the way it would have been put.

But you don't confine yourself, like Robin Hood, entirely to stealing from the aristocracy, Bob, so let's consider another point as well. How do you justify wage-snatches for instance?

Could we get one thing clear first? I'm not trying to 'justify' anything. There's always two points of view on any subject, a wrong one and an even more wrong one. There's so much injustice in the world that we could start swopping one for another all the way along, like me turning round on you and saying: 'You justify some of your respectable society to me—like a managing director of a company taking five thousand a year for himself, from the efforts of people working for him whom he pays five hundred a year'—and so on.

So I'm not justifying anything; I'm just telling you what my point of view on a thing is when you ask me, and my point of view's probably as illogical and wrong as anyone else's is likely to be. I'm not saying: 'This is a hundred per cent right and everything else is wrong.' I'll put my point of view, but you're entitled to disagree with it and so is anyone else—in fact I wouldn't expect you to do anything other than disagree, because you belong in so-called 'straight' society.

Yes, O.K., Bob, but let's just stick to the point, shall we, and save the fireworks. What about wages-snatches?

Sure—but you can't blame me if you leave yourself wide open, can you? All right, wages-snatches. I'll try and take it from the beginning.

If I can see a chance of earning myself—or making myself, if you prefer it—a few thousand quid all at one go, naturally I'll do it. It's only what people, millions of them, are trying to do on the football pools every week. You could say: 'Yes, but they're trying to do it honestly'—to which I'd reply: 'It depends on your definition of honest, because while they're trying to get themselves several thousand of someone else's money for the outlay of a few shillings and no work, I'm trying to get it by some careful thinking and plotting, some bloody hard effort, and the risk of my own liberty into the bargain.'

So who's doing more to earn the money—me or the pools 'investors', as they're called? (By the promoters, of course. It's the old con-man's trick of persuading a mug you're going to give him something for nothing, playing on people's natural avarice and greed.) The 'investors' trust to luck to bring them a lot of money—well, I back on my own efforts.

But there's a difference. Pools winnings come out of what the 'investors' hand over voluntarily, so those who lose have no complaint. Workers don't hand over their wages voluntarily for you to steal.

I'll say they don't. But look, don't try to break my heart. Who loses on a wages-snatch—the workers? Of course not. It's the company—and they can usually stand it. It's the same with banks—if I have a few thousand from a bank, theoretically it's their customers' money I've taken. But you never hear of a bank apportioning the losses round their customers, do you? 'We're so sorry, Major Bloodworthy, somebody blew our safe last night and took ten thousand quid—and it was your ten thousand that was in there!' Mind you, I'm not saying they shouldn't; to me it's quite an attractive idea.

No, let's face it, most of these people are insured against robberies, so it's only the insurance companies who pay up.

But this doesn't in any way defend the use of violence to get it, does it, by coshing the man carrying the wages-bag for instance?

There you go again, using words like 'defend' and 'justify'. I'm trying to tell you I'm not defending it, because fundamentally I don't believe you can defend the use of violence at all, in any circumstances. It's wrong whoever uses it and whatever they use it for. It's wrong when I use it, it's wrong when American maniacs drop an atom-bomb on Hiroshima or Nagasaki, when the South African police shoot down Africans at Sharpeville, when a man commits murder, when 'respectable' society takes him and hangs him as punishment, when Eden orders the British Air Force to bomb Port Said. This is all wrong, every time.

You get this in Parliament a lot, these politicians, usually the Tories, who start steaming off about the increase in crimes of violence, and how 'these thugs have got to be stopped'—these same fellers who were waving their order-papers and dancing up and down with delight when they thought we'd bombed the 'Egyptian wogs' into submission. Who are they to tell me that I'm beyond the pale for using violence?

Bob . . .

Yes, all right. So violence is wrong, on a fundamental level, I admit that. But on a day-to-day level it just happens that it's a tool of my trade and I use it—like an engineer uses a slide-rule, or a bus-driver the handbrake, or a dentist the drill. Only when necessary, and only when it can't be avoided. If I've got to whack a bloke with an iron bar to make him let go of a wages-bag he's carrying, O.K., so I'll whack him. If he lets go without any trouble, I don't. That's all.

I don't indulge in it, you know, for the sheer pleasure of the thing. I'm no sadist. This has always been my theory, that I'll take whatever job comes along. If there's a vanload of stuff to be pulled, I'll pull it; a screwing job, I'll screw it; a safe-blowing, I'll blow it—and so on. And if it's a coshing job, well then, I'll use a cosh.

There's another thing too that I think we ought to get straight. Violence is in a way like bad language—something that a person like me's been brought up with, something I got used to very early on as part of the daily scene of childhood, you might say. I don't at all recoil from the idea, I don't have a sort of inborn dislike of the thing, like you do. As long as I can remember I've seen violence in use all around me—my mother hitting the children; my brothers and sister all whacking one another, or other children; the man downstairs bashing his wife, and so on. You get used to it, it doesn't mean anything in these circumstances.

I've even seen, more than once, two men striping each other with razors—and then, a few nights later, those same two men, with their faces covered with sticking-plaster, drinking together in a pub. I told you about Billy O'Lynn's father, and taking the gun for him, and how he said to us afterwards: 'Just you remember, that's the way to deal with people.' So you see, to me there's nothing all that terrible, or special in any way, about violence. It's just like any other form of activity: eating, sleeping, drinking, screwing, whatever you like.

Perhaps this might sound a bit odd, but it's true—as I've grown older, violence has got divided into two categories for me: the sort that's used for what you might call 'personal' reasons, and the sort to be used on a job.

The first sort, the 'personal' kind, I'm always struggling to get away from. Perhaps it's because I'm getting older or more mature: but I'm reaching the point now sometimes when I'm having an argument with somebody, and feel myself starting to lose my temper, I try and take a grip on myself, say to myself: 'No, I'm not going to whack him, it's wrong, it's sheer bullying, that's all. I've got to use my brains and argue myself out of this.' If I feel I'm not going to be able to do it, I try and make myself walk away from him altogether.

I never carry a knife or anything, no razor, nothing like that now. I used to, and I've used one in my time, striping people I'd got a big personal grievance against: but never light-heartedly, only after thinking about it a lot, and not more than six or eight times at the most. But God forbid, I've given up carrying a chiv now; it's not quite nice, one can so easily become a hooligan.

A few years ago it was different, I'd have whacked anyone soon as look at them, but it's childish, uncivilized, undignified, to be like that. Now, as I say, if I get in an argument, I try to get out of it by walking away. Yet if the selfsame bloke I'm arguing with was walking along the street one day, carrying a wages-bag that I was going to have, of course I'd whack him then. It wouldn't be personal bad temper, you see, only part of the job.

I've almost gone through a complete change-round. When I was a kid I was always looking for a fight. If someone offended me, whoever he was and however big he was, I'd be up to him waving my fists and offering to fight. But it worried me to have to hit someone on a job.

I can remember the first time quite clearly. I was only a kid, sixteen or seventeen, and thought myself a real tearaway of course. There was an old woman, a pawnbroker I think she was, lived in a little house just off Cable Street somewhere. Me and a couple of my mates heard that on Saturday nights she always had a bomb in there. Money was short and we decided to have it.

We went along about nine o'clock one Saturday night with shooters, banging on the door and shouting out: 'Mrs Rosenbloom, Mrs Rosenbloom!' or whatever her name was. 'Let us in, it's urgent, we've got to talk to you.' She opened the door, and seeing we were only kids she let us in. When we were inside we shoved her back into her kitchen and knocked her into a chair, telling her to keep quiet while we turned the place inside out looking for the money.

So of course she starts screaming and raving like a mad woman. Before we went in it'd been decided it was going to be my job to keep her quiet. I rammed my shooter up against her ear and said: 'Belt up, you old faggot, or I'll pull the trigger.'

It made not a blind bit of difference, she just yelled all the louder for help. The other two were tearing everything to bits trying to find where she'd hidden her money, and this racket she was making was really getting on their nerves, so one of them said: 'Oh, for Christ's sake hit the old bag, can't you? If you don't lay her out she'll have the whole neighbourhood on us.'

And I just couldn't do it. All I could do was stand there bleating: 'Shut up, will you! I'm warning you, I'll pull the

95

trigger.' Naturally it didn't stop her. Finally one of the other two walked over, took the gun out of my hand, and belted her unconscious. He put the gun back in my hand, really angry, and he said: 'It's her or us, you silly bastard, can't you see that?'

It taught me the lesson, and after that I was all right. But I've never been keen on the idea of hitting old women, or old men for that matter. Just a personal weakness, but I don't like it, I don't think it's right. Nowadays I don't go in for it at all: if there's a job involving old people, I back out.

Gradually, you see, as you go on, most of the squeamishness about things gets knocked out of you. Not long after the old woman, I was on a job when we had to push around a wages clerk from a supermarket.

He used to be sent every week on his own to the bank to get the money for wages, and then walk back carrying several hundred pounds in a bag. We followed him around for a few trips first, and worked out the best place to stop him—at a corner junction, where he usually had to wait to cross the road. We came up by the side of him in a car, and hauled him in the back. It's better than starting a fight in the street, because sometimes if you do that passers-by try and join in and the thing develops into a rough-house.

I was in the back of the car, holding his face down on the floor so he wouldn't get a good look at us, and knocking him about a bit to make sure he handed over the bag. He did that without much trouble, and I told the bloke who was driving to pull up so I could sling him out.

But the driver wouldn't. He said it was too dangerous to stop, and I should push him out while we were going. It was the attitude of 'him or us' again. So eventually I shoved him out when we were going fairly slowly to get round a corner. Still a bit squeamish, you see, even then.

But not long after that there was another job, in a ware-house in Islington: and this one got rid of the last of my scruples about violence. While we were in the place the night watchman heard us moving about and he came up the stairs to the floor we were on, to see what was going on. On the landing were a couple of five-gallon oil drums. When I saw him coming up towards us, I lifted one of them up right over my head and let him have it. It knocked him back all the way downstairs, but he lay at the bottom yelling blue murder, so I took a fire extinguisher off the wall and went down and laid him out with it. I didn't try to batter him to death or anything, just put him out and stop his noise. I didn't feel angry, savage, anything like that—I don't think I felt anything, just dis-passionate about it, knowing it'd got to be done, because he was threatening us and our safety with his noise.

You felt no compunction at all about hitting him like that?

No, none. I feel if someone takes a job as night watchman he's got to be prepared to be hit if he tries to make a hero of himself. I wouldn't have touched him if he'd left us alone, but since he tried to stop us he got what he'd earned. Personally I think he was stupid, he should have kept quiet and kept his nose out of it. What was he trying to do, win himself a medal? And what was he hoping to get from it, anyway—a pat on the shoulder from the guv'nor, 'Good feller, Jim,' a gold watch when he retired? Anyone who takes a job like that wants his brains testing, to me he does. Perhaps I'm missing something, but I can't see anything admirable in it at all, these heroes trying to win themselves medals for about nine-pounds-ten a week. You read it in the papers sometimes—'Last night Mr Jim Smith tried to tackle some bandits and he's now in hospital recovering from concussion.' It always gives me a laugh, if it was a job I was on that it's referring to. O.K., so the bloke's a hero and got his name in the paper. So what's he got for it? Concussion. And what have I got? What I went for, which is

G

what I would have got anyway, and he needn't have got his concussion trying to stop me.

But it's fortunate not everybody uses your methods, isn't it, or else we'd all be living in the jungle?

But we *are* living in a jungle. You've put your finger on it with that word, though, because that's all it is, a question of method. Lots of people take money off others, but they use other ways of doing it. Some of them are considered respectable. Personally I don't think they are—but it's a matter of opinion, that's all.

A landlord gets money out of people when he puts their rents up, by extortion, by playing on the fact they've got nowhere else to live. And the Law upholds him in doing it. Yet really all he's doing is stealing money from people. But if I go along and steal that money from him he screams to the Law, and they come after me to try and get his money back for him. If his tenant screams to the police that his landlord's robbing him, they do nothing of course. No: he perpetrates his crime upheld by all the respectability of society, without any risk on his part of going to prison. Well, personally, I think my method's a lot more straightforward and honest than his is. And I don't pretend to be doing anything other than what I am—stealing. But the landlord does. And, what's more, I don't go in for robbing poor people either, like he does. Thieving off your own kind, that's terrible.

Or take the case of a jeweller. He's a business man, and he's in the game to make money. O.K., so I'm a business man too, and I'm also out to make money. We just use different methods. The jeweller makes a profit—and often a very big profit—out of what he sells. On top of that he fiddles the income tax and the purchase tax, and even the customs duty as well if he can get away with it. That's considered all right by him and others like him, and if he makes enough to buy himself a big house and a posh car everyone looks up to him as a clever feller, a shrewd business man. But how's he got his money? By rooking people, taking advantage of soft young couples getting engaged to sell them a more expensive ring than they can afford, and fiddling the authorities whenever he can. But at least he didn't steal it. Well, what's in a name? Tell me exactly where the line is between thieving and 'shrewd business' and I might believe it. What's more, the jeweller can insure himself against people like me going and pinching his stock. But I can't insure against the police nicking me, can I? The Law's on one side only, the side of the pretenders, that's all.

It's funny, there's a few criminals, you do meet them from time to time, who won't do any violence. A firm I was with once, there was three of them besides me, we were discussing some job we had in view—a wages-snatch I think it was—where it was obvious we'd have to whack someone to get what we wanted. One of the three was one of these humanitarian types, you know, had what you might call a conscientious objection to using violence altogether. He went on about it so long the other two started to dither as well. We had a long argument about it, and my line was the one I've already explained: if violence needs doing, then you've got to do it. Some people won't hand over to you what you want just like that, so you've got to whack them. Well, this whole job fell through because they didn't look at it my way at all, they were scared about the thing. Once you start drawing lines here, there, and everywhere about what you will do, and what you won't, you might as well give up villainy altogether. It's amateurism—and the amateur's the curse of thieving like he is of any other game. The only approach I can go along with is to be a professional, and get on with whatever comes.

Would being 'a professional' include such a thing as using a gun, for example?

Oh, my good God, no. To any really professional criminal

somebody who uses a shooter is out completely; he's the amateur pure and simple. Only kids do things like that. I did once, when I was young, like I've told you.

I think this is largely the fault of the films and TV, you know—this conventional picture of the hard-bitten gangster with a gun, eyes like steel blots, thin bloodless lips, all that kind of crap. It's an American idea. It might be true in America, I don't know, but certainly I've never met a real criminal like that in my circle of acquaintances, except for an odd hopeless psychopath here and there. But they're very rare. The only people who use guns are scared nervous kids. Otherwise guns are out.

It reminds me of a joke—there's a lot of truth in it—about the tearaway who got himself a gun and burst into a bank with it, holding it in front of himself with two hands to stop anyone seeing how much he was trembling. He glared round at all the counter clerks and he said: 'All right, you stickers— this is an eff-up!'

It's not, as a lot of people might think, because of fear of the penalties, fear of getting topped if you kill someone, nothing like that. If it's killing you're going in for, a knife or an iron bar's better, because at least you can be fairly sure where it's going to land when you use it. But a gun's not reliable. Look what happened to Verwoerd: bloke put the shooter right up against his head before he pulled the trigger, and even then he didn't kill him, only gave him a sore throat for a few weeks.

No, it's nothing to do with fear of the penalty, it's much deeper than that. Psychology comes into it. You see, quite frankly, the British public sicken me where guns are concerned. They're quite incapable of taking them seriously, they've got almost complete contempt for them. You can read about it often enough in the papers. Some mug goes into a post office, waving a gun at the old woman behind the counter, and what does she do? She says: 'Put that away, you silly boy, don't you know it might go off and hurt somebody?' Or else she picks up a two-ounce weight from the scales and throws it at him.

With a gun, you see, three things go through people's minds one after the other when they're threatened with it. The first one is—is it loaded, or is he just bluffing? The second—even if it is loaded, would he really dare to use it? And the third—even if it is loaded, and he would use it, would the bullet hit me or can't he shoot straight?

By the time they've gone through working all that out, they've come to the conclusion the chances all told are better than fifty-fifty against them getting hurt—so they start screaming and throwing things, or pick up a phone and dial 999. Some of them take a risk and go further: they try to tackle the bloke, knock the gun out of his hand, like they've seen on TV, big-hero stuff. But the whole point is, with a gun against them, they've got time to think—and nine times out of ten they think themselves into taking a chance.

But if you use an iron bar it's different. You go into a place waving one of those over your head and with a determined look in your eye, like you're going to clout them as soon as look at them—and they know this is real, they know it's direct. They start to back away automatically, without time to start weighing the situation up. You've got the initiative, you've got them afraid. You crack it down on something, the counter or a chair, splintering the wood—and that really frightens people, when they see you actually hit something with it, because they know the next time it'll come down on their heads, if they don't back up and keep quiet.

What about the suggestion, made by certain people, that the 'cat' should be brought back as a punishment for offences such as robbery with violence? How would that affect your attitude?

Well, it's the old business of deterrence again, isn't it, and you know how I feel about that. It just doesn't operate. When it was in existence the 'cat' was another occupational risk, that's all. I've never had it myself, but I did plenty of things that I would have got it for if I'd been caught. I've met quite a few men who've had it, and up to now I've not met one on whom it had the effect it was supposed to, of putting him off. It's only increased their viciousness and bitterness, so far as I can judge. And in certain cases it's increased their standing in the criminal world, they're quite proud of it and look on themselves like heroes, like—well, like fighter pilots in the Battle of Britain, something of that sort.

I don't think I'd be out of step in saying if it were brought back it wouldn't make any difference to me. If they brought back public executions for sheep stealing, I'd probably go in for stealing sheep. There's something of the challenge in this, you know—daring to do what other people daren't.

What form of punishment does have any effect on you—any at all?

No, that's obvious, surely, isn't it? I can take punishment— in a way I can almost accept it as justified. The only thing that ever worries me is kindness; that gets under my skin a bit sometimes, it perturbs me. I haven't had a lot of it, so perhaps it's because I'm not used to it, but it does worry me all the same. Can I say this again here, though—that I'm not making a plea for more kindness in dealing with criminals. It's quite immaterial to me what method you try—but I think it's probably better for you, it does you less harm, to be kind.

You've explained how you feel about your own use of violence on other people, how you use it as a tool for the job. How do you feel when violence is used against you by others?

That depends on who's using it and what for, and under what circumstances. If I go after a bloke to give him a stripe for something, it's more than likely that if I do stripe him not long afterwards he'll come looking for me, trying to do the same thing back again. I don't object to this, in fact I expect him to do it: I know I'd do the same myself if it was the other way round.

But I think when the police use it for instance—which they quite often do—when they're trying to pin something on you and haven't got enough evidence unless they can get you to confess—well, this I think is wrong. They're supposed to be upholding the Law, not taking it into their own hands. Mind you, an odd beating from the police is just another occupational hazard, so one's got to put up with it, but all the same it doesn't make me respect them any more. They think I'm just a beetle-browed mental defective, but I've got my standards—and I don't go in for beating up people with a gang of my mates, all of us on to him in one room, like they do. I'll fight anyone any fashion he likes, fair fight or foul fight, and, like I said, if he comes off worst I'm not surprised if he comes after me again later, trying to even the score. But when the police give you a beating you can't go and do them up afterwards: you've just go to take it, and from the very people who are supposed to be getting you to lay off violence as a method. I know they've got their problems, the police, like everyone else: but if they're not clever enough to catch you out with all the resources they've got—cars, radio, tip-offs, grasses, forensic scientists, faked-up evidence, the lot—well, it's one-sided enough already without relying on beatings as well.

Mention of grasses reminds me—you can put them on a level with poncing I mentioned earlier as another thing I couldn't ever do. Grasses and ponces are the two lowest forms of animal life. If a straight man is robbed or chivved, some-thing like that, naturally you expect him to scream to the Law, and when the case comes up to go into court and give evidence against you. There's nothing wrong with that: he lives by his standards, you've offended those standards, and he'll do his best to see you get put away for it. That's O.K.

103

You might not like the bloke very much while he's swearing your liberty away in the witness-box, but that's his standard and it's what you've got to expect.

But when one of your own does it . . . I can't find words for this, only obscene ones—I live outside the Law, and I don't turn to it for help when I'm in trouble. If somebody screwed my house I wouldn't scream to the Law about it, because I don't have anything to do with them ever, I look after myself. Sometimes you get a crooked bloke who's been cut in a fight complaining to the Law, and I think it's disgusting. When *he* gives evidence against you, and you know damn' well if the fight had gone the other way he'd have slashed you to ribbons . . . well, you can put down grassing as even lower than poncing, that's where it belongs.

You get grasses in prison too, characters who try to get themselves favours by giving information to the authorities. They're the most universally hated and despised men in the nick. Whenever you read in the papers about a prisoner being attacked by others in a prison, it's usually a safe bet he was a grass. The men who attack him are not the ones who've been grassed either, they're other prisoners trying to uphold the law—their law—the prison law: Thou Shalt Not Grass. I'd do it myself, anytime I was in the nick—I have done it, in fact—given a grass a battering. I don't have to know him, have anything against him personally for something he's done to me. It's one of the things that's got to be done, the grass has got to be taught his lesson. I've done it, and been swagged off to chokey, and lost remission; fair enough. And next time a grass wants doing, I'll be ready to do it again.

This ties in a bit with one other thing I'd like to say on the subject of violence, which is that most violent men I know—people like myself who indulge in it when necessary—are all terribly high-principled and sentimental in a curious, twisted way. I don't know why this should be true, but it invariably is.

You'll usually find that the more vicious a man is the more likely he is to be soft-hearted about women and children—particularly children. I've heard many violent criminals say this, and they mean it very deeply when they're saying it, that they don't want their own kids to grow up like they are, they want to make enough to take them out of the jungle and let them live like decent, upright people. Of course it's not true, they're only kidding themselves, I suppose, but they say it all the same. It's rationalization, that's all—but I don't know why that particular one should be so common in that particular type of criminal.

Bob, to get back to you yourself now . . . was there ever a point in your life when you made a conscious decision to be a criminal?

No, I can't think of one. I remember when I was doing my first lot of bird, I was quite determined I wasn't even going to try and go straight when I got out. I made up my mind that as soon as I was out I was going to get on with the business of having more money for myself, whatever way I had to use to get it. And going out to work for ten or twelve pounds a week wasn't one of the methods I even thought about. But there wasn't any one particular day when I got up in the morning and said: 'I'm going to be a criminal,' like the kid who says: 'I know what I'll do, I'll be a fireman'—nothing like that. I more or less got accustomed to the idea gradually as I grew up, as I've tried to explain in the life-story part.

What really made you a criminal? Do you know?

This is the point, isn't it, where I should lay back in my chair, put my feet up on the mantelpiece, and say: 'I never had a chance!' But it just wouldn't be true. I don't say I've never had a chance, because I have, I've had plenty of chances if I'd wanted to take them. But I never did.

What made me a criminal? . . . I could reel off a whole lot of reasons, but they'd all only be part of the real answer. I'm always afraid of saying circumstances made me what I am, because I don't think they did entirely at all. Seeing my father, a straight man, getting only poverty all through his life for being straight . . . living in an environment where nearly everyone I knew was dishonest, where stealing was a necessity at some times, an adventure at others, but was always acceptable whatever the reason . . . wanting to impress other kids, getting a reputation for being a tearaway . . . seeing the terrifying dreariness of the lives of other people who were 'straight' . . . not being able to face working for a living because I hated the idea of work. . . .

Those were the circumstances, but they were only part of the answer. I still think I'd have been a criminal, whatever they'd been. For one thing, there's this tremendous hatred of authority which I've got, this compulsion, almost, to defy it. I was born with that, I'm sure. Or I could say it was because I'd always had a desire for adventure, for living dangerously. That was true when I was young, but it isn't true now, and I still go on. Now crime's just business, that's all.

There's so many facets, you see, aren't there, to what makes anyone what they are? I don't think there's one reason for me being a criminal, there's many, many of them. Some I know about, some I don't—but they all contribute to a greater or lesser degree. I might say: 'If only I'd had this, that, or the other,' or: 'If this had happened, or that hadn't . . .' My mother dying, for instance, when I was young: that's one example. . . . If I'd been thrashed less, or thrashed more . . . I just don't know. I've never found one answer that convinced me, myself, in my own mind—you know, nothing I could think of and suddenly say: 'Yes, that's why I became a criminal.' I've thought about it a lot for many years and if I did know the answer, the answer you want, and could present it to you like that on a plate—well, I'd be a remarkable man. It seems to me that I've always been a criminal and always will be.

But, you know, you're asking me a question that far better people than me can't even answer. Some of them get paid for sitting in Chairs at universities and trying to work out the answer to this one, don't they? People like Grunhut and Mannheim and Radzinowitz. 'What makes criminals?'— they're working on it all the time, getting paid thousands a year to try and come up with the answer.

I've read a lot of books by those people, articles in the *Journal of Criminology* and so on—after all, crime's the most interesting subject in the world to me, naturally—and none of them know, do they, however hard they try? And they're good people, those people, terrific brains—some of the work they do is first rate. I'm not knocking them, I wish there were more like them, working things out, trying to get other people to think deeply about these things instead of screaming all the time for more beatings, more imprisonment, more punishment. I think that fundamentally they're good and on the right lines. Dr T. P. Morris, he's another one—I've read things of his, heard him on the radio, he knows his stuff, he talks sense.

And, well, sometimes some of them get near some of the answers. But they don't know *the* answer, any more than Lombroso or Alexander Paterson did. They can tell you about conditions, environment, heredity, reactions to treatment of one kind or another—but they still can't tell you why under one set of circumstances some people go bent and others go straight.

Don't get me wrong, I'm all for them hammering away at it. But take any one of them, take—well, let's take Radzinowitz, for instance, he's about the top man now, I suppose, isn't he? I can't help feeling this, that all the time he's working in the dark, he's guessing. Because he's not a criminal himself, and so he can't know.

Hugh Klare, he's another one. That Howard League of his, I think it's an organization working on the right lines: the pursuit of knowledge, that's always a good thing, a fine thing, there are some marvellous people in the Howard League. Even old man Butler, setting up his what-does-he-call-them, his research units on every little aspect of the problem—he's trying too. But there's one thing I think they're all missing, all of them—how do they ever think they're really going to find out what makes criminals tick if they go on looking on criminals just as specimens to experiment on?

You know, you can learn a lot about butterflies by catching one, sticking it on a board with a pin, and looking at it through a microscope. You can study its wing-structure, its anatomy, how it breeds, how it flies, its whole mechanism—but you're still nowhere near knowing what it's like to *be* a butterfly, are you?

Why don't these people sometimes set aside altogether the rights and wrongs of the matter, and get a few criminals to work in with them on the thing of what it's actually like to be one? Those who've given up crime now and reformed, they're no good, they're dead butterflies, their mental processes have atrophied—they've got too far away from it, mentally I mean. But an ordinary criminal, a working criminal, it's my guess if they could only dig down deep enough to find it in him— he'd know just by instinct some of the answers the butterfly inspectors are missing.

To return to yourself now, this feeling you have about being a criminal fundamentally—would it be right to say that in your case not only do you feel this, but, on an even deeper level perhaps, you feel you don't belong in 'respectable' society at all?

Yes, I think that's true. I do feel that now, very strongly. I don't want to mix at all with people who have what might be called 'suburban pretensions' or respectability. They don't interest me: in fact, more than that, I don't like them, I actively dislike them. To me it's much more interesting to be with a group of criminals than a group of suburbanites, because there's nothing about those people at all. I know what they're like, once you've met one you've met them all, you can foretell everything about them right down to the smallest detail. How their homes are furnished—all in the same way: the telly in the corner, lace curtains, a plaster dog in the window, a wooden clock on the mantelpiece, photographs in chromium frames on the sideboard, two armchairs in uncut moquette, four dining-chairs, one of those hideous, glossy cocktail cabinets if they really want to impress . . . they're so stereotyped they're dead. And their talk . . . the man, if you can get down to it, he always 'fancies' the woman next door but of course he never gets round to actually doing her. It's frightening, it's chronic. At least criminals have something interesting to talk about, their talk is deeper and more real, the life they lead goes at a much faster tempo and has got some excitement in it.

I think, if I'm going to try and be strictly honest about this whole thing, that I ought to say, too, that now and again, on some points, I don't feel I belong all that completely in my own strata of society either. I'm not trying to flatter myself and say I'm a cut above them or anything like that— but I do find sometimes, over certain things, that I don't belong.

I can remember before now on more than one occasion, for instance, going into a public library near where I was living, and looking over my shoulder a couple of times before I actually went in, just to make sure no one who knew me was standing about and seeing me do it. You get this in all walks of life, of course, but I must admit a lot of the people I know aren't exactly what you might call 'with it' on some things. I mean, I know blokes who if you mentioned Leonardo da Vinci to them, their first question would be: 'Whose mob's he with?' and if you were to tell them he was a painter, they'd say: 'Well, how much does he make?'

But I think perhaps this isn't all that important anyway, because certain types don't go much on this art business, and I don't look down my nose at them for that. If I had to choose between an art-addict and a sound, reliable screwsman for company, of course I'd choose the screwsman every time. It's the same with a woman—so long as she's reliable, and preferably a good screw into the bargain, that's far more important than she should be clever or things like that.

And yet, if you take you as representative of your strata of society, and me as representative of mine—superficially, at least, we're never short of things to talk about, and we get on. At what points then do we differ; when are you most conscious of the difference?

Well, socially we only touch without embarrassment on a common stamping-ground like a pub or a club or a restaurant. But in your home, for instance, we're poles apart. I always feel this if I go to a straight man's home—if the people know I'm a criminal they won't really accept me: and if they don't know (when you take me to some of your friends', for instance), well, if they did know, they wouldn't accept me.

I'm no more acceptable to your class than you are to mine. This feeling of mistrust would be equally pronounced if I took you round to some of my friends'. How could they feel anything else? You couldn't be trusted to keep your mouth shut about things you might hear. This doesn't mean we'd think you'd go rushing off to the police, nothing like that— but you might happen to mention to another straight person something you'd heard, and he might mention it to someone else, and that person would tell the police. That's the reason for the mistrust, and it's not unreasonable. But a thief knows of one of his own kind that he wouldn't ever take a risk by talking in the wrong places.

And your class of person has got a long way to go, too,

before they ever accept a criminal as anything else but an insensitive second-class citizen. I remember a man coming to see me once, a straight man he was, and he looked along that row of books over there on the shelves, and he said: 'You know, it's really amazing you should read books like this, I'm staggered I am. I should've thought you'd read paper-backed thrillers, things with lurid covers, books like that. And here you are with Claud Cockburn, Hugh Klare, Simone de Beauvoir, and Lawrence Durrell!'

You know, he didn't see this as an insulting remark at all: in fact, I think he thought he was being honest in telling me how mistaken he was. And that's exactly the sort of patronizing you get from straight people if you're a criminal. 'Fancy that!' they say. 'In some ways you're just like a human being!' I'm not kidding, it makes me want to choke the bleeding life out of them.

I've got some justification for feeling, when things like that happen, that people conclude if you've got a Cockney accent you can't be bright, you must be stupid. And if on top of having the accent you're a criminal as well, then that settles it, you must be subhuman into the bargain. When you show a grain of intelligence or interest they're so knocked back they even forget you're insultable, because they never thought you'd got any feelings, so how could they hurt them? It's the same attitude a lot of people have towards coloured people: 'They're not really like us, it doesn't matter how we behave towards them.'

And I always feel this with straight people—that whenever they're being nice to me, pleasant to me, all the time really, underneath they're only assessing me as a criminal and nothing else. It's too late for me to be any different now to what I am, but I still feel this keenly, that that's their only approach, and they're quite incapable of accepting me as anything else.

I know what they think when they meet me. They think: 'Yes, he's a nice feller, that Bob—but I still wouldn't let him marry my daughter, even though he is white!'

I was talking to Frank Norman a little while back, and he was saying the same thing. He said: 'You know, Bob, I like this fame, and I like all the money that comes with it. But I still wish I'd done it by writing about something else than crime.' You see, to everyone he's still 'Frank Norman the Criminal'. He gets invited to parties, all these crummy débutantes throw themselves at him, and then they go home with a big thrill saying to themselves: 'I've been talking to a real, live criminal.' Well, maybe he is a criminal—but all the same, for all that, he's just an ordinary human being, a man like anyone else.

Bob, isn't the person who is most aware of your criminality—far more than anyone else—yourself?

Well, perhaps you've got something there . . . almost. I don't know, I can't analyse myself as deeply as all that. I feel that now, yes, but whether I've always done so I'm not so sure. But I don't need any help in stoking up the feeling nowadays, because, whether I look upon myself like that or not, other people certainly do.

I think you still do stoke it up yourself. Whenever you go anywhere to meet strangers, or even if you go into a strange place on your own, your reaction is always one of mistrust and suspicion, isn't it?

Yes, it is. It's been like this all my life, of course. Whenever I go into a place—a club, a bar, whatever it is—the moment I get inside I start looking round, trying to pick out the person I must go for if there's trouble. I was like that when I first went into the dining-room at the approved school, I remember, and am now when I go down on association after I've got to prison. Not who do I like, or who do I not like, but—who's the person I must hit if trouble starts? Outside in a pub now, I'll still do this trick of pouring my beer out and leaving a bit in the bottle so the waiter can't take it away, to keep the bottle handy in case there's trouble.

This reaction is like all the others, isn't it—and they're all an expression of the same characteristic? This mistrust, this readiness to resort to violence, this expectation of it almost—it all indicates the same thing surely: fear?

I suppose that's true. I'm not frightened of violence, I don't run away from it—in fact, when I feel it's got to come, I hope it comes quickly and we can get on with it.

Certainly I'm afraid of people analysing me, yes, because I feel they're going to use it against me. And I hate this, because I'm naturally secretive . . . it's ridiculous, but when I've been fooling around sometimes, drawing out on a piece of paper the sort of house I'd like to build myself if I ever had the money—I always plan secret rooms in it, rooms that no one else would know about except me.

I'm afraid of weakness, of showing weakness, most of all. You know . . . I like that Tchaikowsky thing, *The Sugar Plum Fairy*, and I like those daffy, childish paintings by Duouanier Rousseau; but I never tell people that, because they'd think I was soft. Or I'll see a tree in the sunset, with the play of light and shade in its branches, the impressive beauty of it like that—but I can't bring myself to say anything about it to someone if they're with me at the time. I'm afraid they'll think me weak, I'm afraid they'll ridicule me for it, I can't trust what their reaction's going to be. So instead I build up an antagonism towards them, it's quicker and more simple. Other people's opinions shouldn't matter, I suppose, but they do—or, rather, they do and they don't. If they're people I like and who matter to me, it does matter. If I don't like them, I don't give two hoots what they think, in fact I'll go out of my way to encourage their bad impression of me.

Bob, if you could change yourself in any way, lose just one characteristic, which one would it be?

H   113

This . . . this thread of violence that's run all through my life, this broad streak of primitiveness, that's the one big thing I'd like to get rid of. I don't mind being a criminal, I don't think anything'll ever change that now—but the viciousness that goes with it, that does worry me quite a lot now and then. It's the same thing I've got, almost, that you can see on the faces of the spectators at a boxing or wrestling match, if you watch them instead of the ring. I suppose it was there on the faces of the spectators watching the gladiators in ancient Rome, too—this dreadful satisfaction and enjoyment of other people's pain.

Sometimes I feel if I could only get a new slant, a new philosophy, if I used my brain more and my physical strength less, I might get rid of these inadequacies. Because I know they're all wrong—but, you see, I've got nothing else to put in their place. . . .

Like you, I want to know 'Why'—why I'm like this, what it is in me that makes me like this. I give myself all the answers why I'm a criminal, why I'm a violent criminal, but I still know they're not *the* answer. And if I did know, if I knew the true one, the real one—not what Hugh Klare knows or Butler knows, not even what Leon Radzinowitz knows—if I knew that, I'd be a very great and valuable man. Why am I—I? God knows I ask myself often enough, Tony, and the answer is . . . I still don't know.

3

Those who Tried
to Reform

Obviously throughout your life many people have tried, all in their own different ways, to reform you and get you to go straight. Yet none of them ever came anywhere near succeeding.

What was it about them, about their method of approach—and about you yourself—that caused everyone to fail?

Mother

Father

School Teacher

Magistrate

Approved School Headmaster

Psychologist

Prison Officer

Church Army Captain

Class Instructor

D.P.A. Committee

Probation Officer

Chaplain

Barrister

Prison Visitor

Prison Welfare Officer

Psychiatrist

Yᴏᴜ ᴋɴᴏᴡ, all my life it's been questions, as long as I can remember. Why do you do, or feel, this; why don't you do, or feel, that? Always those same questions, loaded with implications and advice, bearing down like a ten-ton truck on a flower-bed, flattening any feelings I might have, skidding across them, uprooting them as though they were unimportant weeds . . . these road-hog, articulate truck-drivers who are so sure they've got the right of way.

You get immune to good advice. Sometimes I resent it, other times it bores me. As a matter of fact, you're the only person I've ever known that I've even thought it worth the effort of really trying to answer properly, that I've ever felt I could entrust my feelings to. I feel you've got the interest of really wanting to know, and aren't trying to get back at me with how right you are and how wrong I am. With most people there's usually been an axe in it somewhere—either to be ground or to be held over my head.

It's not easy for me. I've got conditioned long ago to the answer-pattern of 'Yes—no—maybe—O.K., whatever you say'. We'll take them one by one. Some of them won't answer the question, some of them'll tell you nothing about the people, but perhaps a bit about me. With some it was a case of us both getting off on the wrong foot, with others we were never on any sort of footing at all. With others again, I just don't know. But I'll try. . . .

———

MOTHER

She'd have gone on all her life trying to keep me straight, my mother would, if she'd lived. When I was a kid she always gave me a hiding when she caught me doing anything wrong: the older I got, the harder she laid it on. And there was more to it than just punishing me—I was her boy, and she wanted me to grow up the right way so she could be proud of me, and I could be proud of myself.

I know, without any doubt at all, she loved me more than anyone else in the world did. It gave me a lot of pain whenever she found me out, to know I'd let her down—and I think, if she'd gone on living, I'd probably have felt much worse about a lot of the things I've done.

But even up to the time of her dying she hadn't made much impression as far as keeping me straight was concerned, though it wasn't for want of trying. All her life she'd more than her share of worry and trouble, and she couldn't cope with half of it because she hadn't the mental equipment to do it. Fundamentally she was a simple person, who loved her husband and her children but who was surrounded by difficulties that anyone, whoever they were, would have found too many and too great, so she concentrated on loving and caring to the best of her ability.

I loved her, and wanted to keep her loving me. If even she couldn't make any difference to me, what chance was there for anyone else?

FATHER

When I got older and started going to prison my father, when he came to see me or wrote to me, used to say: 'Well, it's no use me going on at you, is it, because you know what I think, and you're too old now for me to have much influence.'

This was his expression, in a kind way, of his disappointment in me—and, after all, he'd got good reason to be disappointed, because he'd spent all his life when I was younger trying to influence me to his way of thinking.

But the sense of having disappointed him never weighed very heavily with me at any time in my life—I didn't have the same feeling for him I did for my mother, that I didn't want to let him down, it never mattered half so much. It wasn't that I was antagonistic towards him, nothing like that, but somehow we hadn't much affinity in the way we looked at things. This isn't to say we didn't like or respect each other, because we did—but we never quite matched up in our outlooks.

As far as I can remember, he hit me only once in the whole of my life. He was a very strongly built man, physically very powerful, but he hated to use his strength because he felt one should always try to prevail by reasoning alone. When I did anything wrong he'd try to get me to see I ought to behave differently, pointing out the consequences, how I'd hurt other people, and so on. Except on this one occasion. I'd been cheeky to my mother and I didn't stop when he told me to, until finally he gave me a terrific back-hander that knocked me right across the room. As soon as he'd done it he was terribly upset about it—he thought he'd half killed me because he knew his own strength and it frightened him. After that he never used physical violence on me again.

It would be easy, looking back, to say: 'He ought to have done this, or he ought to have said that.' But whatever it was, I don't think it would have made much difference, because his influence on me wasn't strong.

It's true of both my parents—they never gave up loving me and trying to change me. But the environment in which we lived, and my own nature, both affected me to a far greater extent. My parents were fighting a losing battle all the time against those other influences. When my mother died it wasn't possible for my father to spend a lot of time with me because he was being moved around on war work and his children were scattered all over the place. Yet, even if he had, I don't believe it would have altered me. I had more admiration for my grandfather than I had for him. There was a man I could understand—but my father, he got nothing for all his fruitless, slogging years, and this was what we could never see eye to eye on. It's a curious thing—if he hadn't been straight he might have got somewhere: but, being straight, he never did.

SCHOOL TEACHER

There was one school teacher, and only one, who tried kindness with me at school, instead of reaching for the cane when trouble began, like all the others.

She was a middle-aged spinster, plain, nothing about her at all except the kindness of her face, and I have the feeling she was probably the only teacher who ever liked me. I'm not complaining about the others, though, because I know I was a dreadful little bastard all the time and it wasn't surprising they reacted the way they did. But this woman for some reason took it differently. I think she felt I needed sympathy and understanding, and hoped if she gave it that would get me to change.

I don't know if they still do this in schools, but at that time on Armistice Day the whole class had to stand in silence for two minutes at eleven o'clock. This was always a very serious occasion. We had talks on the subject for several days beforehand, and were told what Armistice Day meant, what the two minutes' silence was for, how all over the country everyone at that time would be stopping whatever they were doing, the traffic would come to a standstill, everything would go quiet and everybody be standing in remembrance for those who'd been killed. That year, whichever it was, I forget now, throughout the whole country everyone was standing silent and still at eleven o'clock—except, I suppose, one small boy in a corner of a school in Shoreditch. He was giggling noisily and reefing the girls.

When the silence was over and we all sat down I looked to see if she was going to call me up for punishment as I expected. But she was sitting at her desk with her eyes full of tears, trying to pull herself together to get on with the lesson. I suppose she must have lost someone in the Great War: her father, her brother, perhaps even her lover, the only one she'd ever had in her life. She'd been so upset by the silence she hadn't noticed my playing about, or, if she did, hadn't thought it worth paying attention to because she was too involved in her own grief.

I think she must have noticed, all the same, because after class she told me to stay behind. When she talked to me then, she never said anything about what I'd been doing during the silence, but she spoke generally about school, trying to get me to trust her and tell her why I hated it. I remember her saying I had to accept there'd always be somebody higher up than me who had the right to tell me what to do, and how she tried to tie it up with herself and the headmaster as an example, how he could tell her what she had to do.

It was a bit involved for a child to follow, I suppose, but my attitude then was: 'Well, the headmaster's your problem, don't ask me for sympathy about it.' She rounded it off by telling me she was going to make me a class monitor—and from then on it was my job to hand out the books, pencils, and paper, clean the blackboard, tidy up the classroom, and so on.

I hated her for that, for putting me in the terrible, embarrassing position of 'teacher's favourite' in the eyes of the rest of the class. This was the good old idea of giving the rebel responsibility. All it did to me was to make me behave worse until she had no alternative but to sling me out from the position of honour.

Even at that age, nine or ten, I was firmly set on my own course of being the unredeemable rebel. We had to write a sort of essay once, I remember, on 'The Life of a Shilling'. Of course mine had to be the life of a counterfeit shilling, not an ordinary one like everyone else's.

This teacher packed up soon afterwards, went to another school, and that was that.

MAGISTRATE

I've already said quite a bit about Basil Henriques, and it's just possible he might have had something with his idea of getting me into the Merchant Navy, if it had come about quick enough.

But I think where he made his mistake—though he can't be blamed for this—was in relying on what other people told him about these hostels he kept sending me to. You very often get this with enlightened people—they have a tendency to think everyone else is up to their own standard of outlook. They make all these efforts and arrangements for you to be looked after, and then the people who actually do it are of nothing like the same calibre, and fall down on it.

Henriques was a busy man, and it's stupid to suggest he should have done it all himself—taken me to the hostel, seen I was O.K., called in every day to make sure I was happy— I'm not suggesting ridiculous things like that. But although he could see how I ought to be handled, it wasn't the same thing as how I actually was handled. On the other hand, of course, you've got to set against that the fact that he didn't know how difficult I was going to be about it all either—so, with a combination of the two factors, his idea never got past its early stages.

But he did make a big effort for me and with me, and I'll always be grateful for that. I look back on Basil Henriques with respect—quite frankly he's the only person in judicial authority that I've ever had any feelings whatsoever for, other than hatred and contempt.

What more can I say about this man Charles Wathen that can add to what I've already said? If his scheme had gone a bit further, and I'd gone on to the technical college like he was trying for, things might have been different—and, of course, they might not. I got called up into the Army, so we never found out.

In a way, he was the last of what might be called 'civilian' triers—those who weren't in some sense closely connected with the prison system. I always had the feeling with him he wasn't just doing a job; he really, personally, cared, not only for me but for all the boys he had under him. And he got this far: that when I went to Carlton I was defiant, full of hatred for the place and for him because he ran it, and when I left, for him, at least, I felt respect. He trusted me, when he'd no safe reason to, and he ran risks in showing it that could have got him into a lot of trouble.

Sooner or later I'd have had to leave Carlton, even if it hadn't been for the Army, and there's no telling anyway what would have happened then. But I'd almost admit that while I was there Wathen did to some degree at least get somewhere with me, certainly further than anyone else: it was his trusting me that did it, and his overlooking of the few occasions when I let him down.

No one else has ever come anywhere near him.

He's retired now, and must be able to spend his time looking back on a lot of successes. Here's one of his failures who looks back at him, and sends him a nod.

PSYCHOLOGIST

This was the first of the 'system' ones, and maybe it set the tone of my reactions to all the others who came afterwards.

She was a woman psychologist in one of the prisons I was in on remand in the early days, and I was sorted out—I don't know who by or what for—to go and be interviewed by her. She had me in her office and told me to sit down while we had a chat 'to see if she could help'.

She wore one of those black cloche hats and a dull, brown coat with a piece of mangy fur round the collar. In age she must have been a bad sixty, I should think; with a voice that creaked like old furniture, a white face, and glittering black eyes. They were the only living things about her, those eyes; they seemed to bore into you as she talked, trying to make you keep your gaze fixed on her.

I was only young and, as I say, all this had been introduced under the general heading of 'help'—so what followed rather knocked me back. She took particulars of where I'd lived, my mother and father and brothers and sisters—and then she was off, staring at me with those eyes of hers, leaning forwards, shooting out questions as though she was jabbing me with a rapier.

—When I was a child did I sleep in the same room as my mother and father?

—No.

—Where did I sleep then?

—In the other room.

—Who with?

—Some of my brothers and sisters.

—All in the same bed?

—No, we were divided up.

—When I slept with my brothers, did I play with them?

—Oh, yes, we were always skylarking about and fighting and diving under the bed and . . .

—No, that wasn't what she meant at all.

She gave me a very piercing look. What she had really meant was, did I ever *play* with them?

I gathered the first answer, yes, had been wrong, so naturally I said no instead. She grimaced.

—And did I sometimes sleep with my sisters?

—Yes.

—Well, did I *play* with them?

—Oh, yes, I was for ever pulling their hair and kicking
them and . . .

She tapped on the desk with her hand impatiently: obviously
she would have to be less subtle.

—Did I ever . . . fondle . . . my sisters?

I began to cotton on to what she was driving at. It made
me very embarrassed to realize it. When I answered no I
could almost read the reaction like a signboard over her head
. . . he looks embarrassed when he says no, so he must really
mean yes.

She pressed on, her eyes boring deeper and deeper. I was
shifting around uneasily in my chair, because I'd become
quite convinced in my own mind she was only a dirty-minded
old woman out for kicks. I couldn't find the answers I needed,
the diplomatic ones which would glide me over the situation,
and this made me resentful and angry; I felt she was an old
person taking advantage of a young and inexperienced one—
inexperienced in talking I mean. My answers got shorter and
even more stupid.

—Had I got any girl friends?

—No.

—Did I have boy friends then?

—No.

—Hadn't I ever had a girl friend?

—No—well, yes, sort of.

—What did I mean, sort of? What did I do with her when
I had had one?

—Went to the pictures.

—But what did I *do* with her in the pictures?

—Looked at the pictures, what else?

—Never held her hand, even?

—No.

—So really I was frightened of girls, was I?

I couldn't help it then, I had to laugh. So she changed to a direct attack in retaliation.

—Had I ever had intercourse with a girl?

—Oh, no. (What a Tom Pepper.)

—Had I ever *wanted* to have intercourse with a girl?

—Oh, no, never. (I was hoping she might ask me did I know what 'intercourse' meant. No such luck.)

—Well, did I ever masturbate?

—No, of course not, never.

The harder she pressed the more pure and unblemished I became, until the score sheet must have totted up to me being a sexless skin bag of grotesque purity. It's a wonder she didn't tell me to take my pants off just to check I wasn't lacking something.

Eventually she sat back with a sigh and rang for a screw to take me away.

What help that whole thing was supposed to be to me I've never yet worked out. The only person it can possibly have benefited was her, so she could work off a few of her own frustrations; that's all it could have done. Throughout the interview the expression on her face was the same as I saw on the face of a very posh-spoken A.T.S. girl once in a Naafi canteen in Germany, when she was reading a pornographic paper-back. 'Oh, my God, how revolting this is, I can't put it down.'

It seems to me this old faggot was the sort you do meet now and then, who harp away on your sex life because they get some sort of vicarious pleasure out of the subject themselves —because they've spent what time they could, when the opportunity presented itself, of having sexual intercourse, but they've never had a good screw in their lives.

PRISON OFFICER

The whole idea of a screw trying to reform someone, let's face it, is ridiculous—but I did meet one once who took it on himself to try. He started off by saying one night as he was banging me up in my cell: 'You're too young to be in these places, boy.' Probably he was right, but as it was the judge who'd put me there it might have been more to the point if he'd told him.

This screw was an oldish sort of geezer, fifty or so, with a red face and crinkly grey hair. You can't expect me to say much complimentary about screws, naturally, so all I'll say about him is there was less to dislike than most, but he was still a screw for all that.

Sometimes in the evenings he'd come along to my cell and unlock me on some pretext or other, just so he could have a few minutes' chat with me. After a time he started bringing in books for me to read. I must have told him once about this Merchant Navy lark I'd been thinking of, because two of the books he brought me were by Captain Marryat— *Masterman Ready* and *Mr Midshipman Easy*. They'd both been written—what, a hundred years ago?—so I wasn't exactly impressed. They were kids' stuff, not up to my usual standard of reading matter by then—Hank Janson, Ben Sarto, and other literary greats.

This old screw had been in the Army twenty years himself, and used to tell me what a great life it was. He was a simple-minded sort of man, and thought things that had made an impression on him would make an impression on me, which of course they didn't. One of his arguments was: 'If you've got brains enough to work out a robbery, you've got brains enough to find yourself a decent job.' Like all great philosophies, it was simple: but, like any kind of philosophy, it didn't appeal to me. I used to agree with his points as he made them, and then he'd go off thinking I seemed a decent enough lad because I knew sense when I heard it. What was the alternative to agreeing, anyway? I didn't want to have long discussions with him, because it looks bad if you spend too much time talking to a screw.

CHURCH ARMY CAPTAIN

I've never gone a lot on the Church Army, because my early experiences of it, in the person of the captain at the hostel who tried to choke me, hadn't endeared me to it. As I got older, and my experience widened—every prison has its resident Church Army captain—my dislike developed into contempt. They trot round in their natty little grey uniforms, being terribly jovial all over the place, and it's all so unreal, so forced, it makes you cringe. They remind me of the nineteen-twentyish character in plays—you know, the one who comes in through the french windows in a blazer and white flannels saying: 'Who's for tennis?' These characters go around in the same way, almost, saying: 'Who's for Jesus?'

One came to see me once when I was down in the punishment cells doing three days' bread-and-water. It was the middle of winter; one of the panes in the window the other side of the bars was broken, and it had been snowing hard outside so quite a lot of the snow had got blown into the cell. He came bursting in when I was lying on my mail-bag: 'Good evening, good evening!' all over the place. I could see from the frown on his face he thought I ought to have stood up when he came in, instead of just lying there looking at him.

'Well,' he said, 'and how are you getting on?'

'Oh, marvellous,' I said, looking at the snow in little drifts on the floor.

'Good, good,' he said. 'That's the spirit!' Then: 'Have you

asked permission to go to Chapel on Sunday? You can do, you know, if you want to.'

'No, I haven't.'

'Then why don't you?' he said. 'It'd make a bit of a break for you, you know, wouldn't it?'

'No,' I said, 'I'd sooner stay here.'

He looked down at me, very seriously. 'Always a trouble-maker, you are, aren't you?'

'Look,' I said. 'I'm not making any trouble. I'm just staying down here nice and quiet, freezing to death. So where's the trouble?'

He didn't like that, they never do, and off he went with a long lecture about mending my ways and repenting, and not having to think myself better than everyone else all the time. It was O.K. for him, five minutes later he'd be warming his arse in front of a roaring fire in the screws' clubroom, tut-tut-ing and shaking his head over how difficult I was and what a hard time he had trying to get all these bad people to see the light.

He'd come to see how I was getting on. Well, I wasn't getting on, I was cold and hungry and miserable—but he didn't do anything to put it right, all he was hoping was I'd be sufficiently cowed in spirit to go to his service on Sunday. Redemption through suffering. The only thing that warmed me from his visit was the raging contempt I had for him. They make me sick, these preaching humbugs.

CLASS INSTRUCTOR

There was a woman once, used to take English classes in one of the prisons I was in. Not exactly young—thirty or forty perhaps, which was a good deal older than me then—but quite good-looking, with a quiet manner and a lot of sincerity. Her classes were always a bit of a circus, because she kept no sort of discipline; there were dice games going on, all the poofs reefing one another, that sort of thing. She used to encourage me to write, and as writing was one thing I was keen on we struck up quite a sort of understanding. She'd come and sit next to me in class and talk over an essay or some other thing I'd written, and criticize it constructively, encourage me to try and express myself in my own way.

Of course I got a lot of leg-pulling from the others about it, they were always telling me she fancied me, but I put up with it because I knew it wasn't true. She used to tell me it was a terrible waste, me being in prison, because I had talent if only I'd stick at writing, and work on it. Naturally I'd no confidence in my ability to do it when I got out of prison, so one day she said: 'When you come out, why don't you come and live at my house for a while, settle down to writing without any worry about jobs or where you're going to live? I've got plenty of room, no one will bother you, you could live there and write as much as you wanted to.'

What finished it was when she told me about all the famous people she knew—writers, painters, composers—and how she'd take me round and introduce me to them. It was my impression—and maybe I was wrong—that all she wanted to do was keep me as her little lap-dog and tour me around, showing off her great big he-man criminal to her friends.

She was far too clever to give me straight, good advice, but she did play quite successfully for a time on my own feelings of vanity.

D.P.A. COMMITTEE

Committees of the Discharged Prisoners' Aid Societies are supposed to look after your welfare when you come out of prison. The general opinion of all prisoners is that these organizations are not worth a carrot. From a criminal's point of view they're shocking, they're pathetic, they're sneered at, and I've never heard a single prisoner say a good word or a kind word for them yet.

You used to have to come up in front of them before you left prison. The interviewing board usually consisted of a couple of pompous do-gooders, men of local importance, and an odd parson or two thrown in. They sat there smug and self-important, and they seemed to think that if they gave you something, half a crown or five bob, it was coming out of their own pockets. And if they gave you advice—which costs nothing—they always gave it in a very patronizing way. 'What you should do is this, that, and the other, go here, go there,' and so on. They were all the time telling you what they thought you should do, and weren't interested in your point of view at all. They knew best and that's all there was to it. You just couldn't find an affinity, a basic level, on which you could discuss your problems with people like that.

Most self-respecting prisoners wouldn't even dream of approaching the D.P.A. for help because they know it would be useless, they've tried it before, and they've heard not once but hundreds of times, from other prisoners, how hopeless the whole set-up is.

You know, when they're contemplating what it's going to be like when they leave at the end of their sentence, most prisoners evaluate pictorially. They see themselves going in front of the D.P.A. and being questioned about what they're going to do, where they're going to live, what sort of job they're going to find, having good advice thrown in—'Oh, you shouldn't do that, you ought to do this'—and the most they'd come out with at the end is a letter for the National Assistance Board.

So on the morning you're released you trot off with your letter. And you think about going into the local office of the N.A.B., waiting in a queue, and then some woman at the counter (I don't know why one should always visualize a woman in this, but you do: always a woman, and always the same type, the glacier sort), when you get up to your turn she opens the letter and frowns, and then she says: 'Hm, well, where do you live? I don't know if we can do anything for you, sit down over there and we'll see.'

Of course you always take the pessimistic outlook that she's going to be no use to you—and usually you're right. After hours of sitting around waiting, eventually she tells you to go to the Labour Exchange and get a Form B-Oblique-Stroke-Twenty-nine-Dash-Thirty, or something fantastic like that. Off you go to get this, often to a Labour Exchange which is miles away, and you have to wait hours again there: and then back to the N.A.B. with the form, and more waiting and waiting. All for thirty bob.

This is the picture you conjure up: Offices with their institutional décor, the hard bench seats; the woman who never changes, who's always this glacier type; and the bossy, pompous sort of man they have there as well, who asks you questions in a loud voice, broadcasting all over the place you've just come out of prison; and all the agony of the eternal wait. 'Well,' you think, up there in your cell, 'my God, I've seen enough of these bastards in here, without going outside to meet them as well.'

So you don't put down for the D.P.A. You know when you get out one of your friends will always lend you a fiver straight off, without any questions or form-filling or good advice.

PROBATION OFFICER

To be fair, I must say the probation officer who had most to do with me when I was under him on licence after my Corrective Training made no great effort to reform me. From the start he accepted me for what I was: I suppose he thought he could make more profitable use of his good advice on others. It was mostly a case when he saw me of: 'Hello, how are you, where are you living, are you still working? Yes, well, you're O.K.' Even when it was obvious I wasn't working, he didn't much want to know.

Yet there were times when I went to see him and we had long talks and arguments about politics, books, the world situation, things like that. But never about my after-care. He had a habit, this bloke, of putting on an air of familiarity, of being 'one of the chaps', who knew it all and was just like you himself. This is a common way of trying to win confidence, and it gets nowhere: in fact it gets less respect than that of the outright, upright prude.

I've met a few others at other times in my life, or when this one was away, and they usually fall into some similar recognizable type. There are hearty back-slapping ones who use words like 'bloody' and 'bugger' to show they've got the common touch. There are very earnest ones who've got a vocation for it, whom you hurt much more than you hurt yourself—they imply—when you let them down. There are the real tough-guys who've heard all these tales before and won't have the wool pulled over their eyes—they're all right in dealing with kids, perhaps, who might take them at their own valuation. There are the very deep ones, who think hard as they pull at their pipes but say nothing, usually to cover up the fact they can't think what to say. There are frighteners who tell you how much bird you'll do next time, threateners who say how much trouble they can get you into, pleaders who complain you're messing up the way they run their office. . . .

About the only thing they've got in common is that they all know better than you what you should do, and they all know exactly how you should do it.

'Now look, what you ought to do, son, is go and get a job labouring for a few weeks—anything, it doesn't matter what sort of a job it is—so you can earn yourself a few pounds. But don't spend it, live on thin air instead, and save up the money to buy yourself a decent suit. Then, when you've got that, you can go and get yourself a better job and earn more money to save up and buy yourself two suits. So in six months' time you'll have two smart suits and a pair of winkle-pickers.... Of course, you might have died of starvation and boredom in the meantime, but never mind.'

And if you turn round and say: 'Well, if you think it's such a marvellous idea, why don't you go out labouring and living in a doss-house? At least then you'd really know what you were talking about.'—if you do that, they write on your card in their little filing-box: 'Difficult, aggressive, unco-operative. Will come to a bad end.'

None of these probation officers have got even one step along the road yet with me.

CHAPLAIN

There's still this old idea persists in some quarters that a prison chaplain is some sort of spiritual adviser and confidant to men in prison. Actually it'd be hard to imagine anything further from the truth.

The chaplain in a prison is usually nothing more than a glorified Entertainments Officer. The only people who ever have any time for him are usually, curiously enough, either men who are in for sex offences, or homosexuals. Church service is an opportunity for them to sit next to some other poof they fancy.

The chaplains themselves fall into two main classes—those who are indifferent to the men and pity themselves for the rotten job they've got, and those who think they were specially chosen by God to lecture the downfallen on the error of their ways. They expect prisoners to be frightened of them, playing on the old religious-superstition business.

I remember once putting down to see the padre after I'd been on chokey for hitting a screw. Naturally the other screws had come down and given me a going-over, and I'd decided to complain. I needed some evidence, and thought the nearest thing I'd get to an outside witness in a prison was the Holy Joe. I was standing in line outside his office with a few others, waiting for him to turn up, when he suddenly appeared along the corridor behind us. 'Stop that talking, you men!' he shouted. 'What do you think this is, a holiday camp?' and stamped past us into his office. That sort of talk is no different from a screw's.

When I got in to see him it was the usual business. 'Name and number?' and then, when I'd given that: 'Well, what do you want, be quick!'

'I wanted you to look at these cuts and bruises on me, because I'm going to complain to——'

'Outside!' he yelled at the screw standing by my side. 'Take him out and bring the next one in!'

That was as far as it got. Next Sunday, because I'd nothing better to do, I went to his service, and I remember how worked up he got in his sermon on the subject of Mary Magdalene. His face was red, and he was sweating as he thumped his fist on the edge of his pulpit: 'And Mary Magdalene was a whore, I tell you, a filthy whore. . . .'

Well, I've known a few parsons and I've known a few whores, and I've always preferred the whores.

BARRISTER

There was a bloke appearing for me once on a dock brief, and while we were waiting for the verdict he decided to have a go at me. He told me I was too bright to be spending my life in this way, I ought to pull myself together and get out of crime.

My reaction to him was: why should he choose to try and sort me out—why not the case he defended before, or the one he was going to defend next? Why pick on me? His job was to put up the best case he could, get me off the charge if it was possible, and that was as far as he had the right to go. Just because he was defending me, that didn't give him a free hand to dish out advice as well. As it happened, he didn't get me off: I got three years, plus a lecture from the judge about what he'd give me next time I came up in front of him, which is a thing judges are very fond of telling you when they're sitting up there in judgement and you can't answer back.

But this barrister geezer, he was going to draw his fee and then he was going home to his wife and kids after a hard day's work, while I was off to stew in the nick for three years—so what good did he think he was going to do to me in those circumstances? What he wanted to be able to say was: 'Well, I told him.' All right, he told me: but there's lots of things I'd like to have told him too, like how he wasn't much good at his job.

PRISON VISITOR

I had one of these once, to help pass the time away while I was doing a three stretch. An amiable sort of old boy used to come in and see me for a chat. He'd sit down and say: 'Well, how are we tonight?' but never stop for an answer, just ramble on about this and that. He had a funny trick of inter-rupting himself soon after he'd started, like: 'When I was coming here tonight, I got off the bus and just as I was crossing the road—— Well, I mustn't bore you with that.' Or: 'My wife was saying to me the other day when we were having tea with the children: "Now, George," she said, "I want you to——" But it doesn't matter, it's not important what she said.'

He was a bit of a religious chap, used to tell me (in half-phrases, naturally) about what was going on at his church and so on, and once in a while he'd come out with the old hymn-slinging. 'Don't you think, old chap, that if only you let God——' But then he was true to form and interrupted himself: 'Oh, well, never mind, this isn't really the right time for that.'

As I got to know him better, I began to see he was something of a twisted bastard, too, like a lot of these do-gooders. He was telling me once about some trouble they'd had in a youth club he was connected with, how the warden of it had confiscated some 'dirty pictures' one of the boys had been caught showing round. This old geezer said: 'And, you know, I've knocked about the world a bit, seen a few things in my time, but these photographs they were really dreadful, I've never seen anything so vile, so disgusting.'

'Were there many?' I said.

'Oh, yes,' he said. 'There were twenty-seven.'

'All the same?'

'No, all different poses, every one.'

Another time he was talking about a woman he'd had to go and see, something to do with welfare work he was on. 'She was sitting down, you know, on a chair while we were talking, and I could see she wasn't a clean sort of person at all. I couldn't help noticing her—what do you call it, under her skirt, her underslip, that's it—it was dirty, you know, really very dirty, and all the time I was thinking to myself: "Well, what sort of state must this woman's body be in, what must it be like?" I couldn't help feeling it, you know what I mean?' This was the sort of thing he had to drag up, he had to start telling me the story so he could bring it in—it was a sort of compulsion he had to tell me things like that, because under-neath all his doing good he had a really dirty mind.

And it was himself all the time, what he felt and thought that mattered, not what I did; that was of no interest to him at all. One time he came down to see me when I was on chokey, I'd been put there for fighting with another prisoner, and when he sat down he said: 'Why don't you tell me all about it?'

I started to, but after I'd been going a few minutes I could see his eyes wandering vaguely all round the cell and he wasn't listening any more. I stopped what I was saying, which he didn't notice I should think for a good thirty seconds, then he pulled himself together and said: 'Well, spare a thought for the other fellow, old chap!'

So what's the use of people like this, what do they hope to achieve? In his case, only some sort of self-satisfaction, a feeling he was doing good in the world by giving up a bit of time to convicts—but nothing for them at all, that never came into it.

PRISON WELFARE OFFICER

These are the latest gimmick in a long dreary series of attempts at reforming prisoners by the Prison Commissioners. They've realized the D.P.A.s are a washout, so they've started putting welfare officers in prisons to see if they can do any better on the personal-interview gambit, instead of bringing you up in front of a committee. The result in the end is just the same.

These people are part of officialdom, and the more they keep out of my life the better I like it. They've been running my life for me while I'm in prison, but once I get outside my life's mine. Why should they tell me where to go and what to do, what's it to do with them? I'm not going to be under any obligation when I get out: their right to interfere finishes the moment I step out of the gate.

Their approach varies with who's doing it. One once had me in his office, told me to sit down, gave me a cigarette, and then said: 'Well, what are we going to do?' I said: 'I'm going to do three years, what are you going to do? Perhaps you'd like to do half of it for me, would you?' He slung me out and that was that.

PSYCHIATRIST

I've met a few of these, one time and another. Their favourite line is to give you intelligence tests so they can get you tabulated into some sort of category. They have their categories all set out, and you've got to fit into one of them otherwise they get confused.

I've done these tests of theirs, often, all this nonsense of bricks and blocks, fitting coloured shapes of paper into squares, picking out the odd one from lists like 'Fish-and-chips, steak-and-kidney pie, staircase'. All that sort of rubbish. I always do them wrong deliberately, but of course these people know you do it and pay no attention. I don't know why, but for some reason, when I do them wrong, I still give something away because they carry on with me despite that.

You do the test, and then go into the psychiatrist's office. He tells you to sit down, and says something like: 'You know, you're really quite an intelligent chap, I can tell from your tests.' Up to there we're doing fine, because I think if he can see I'm intelligent he must be quite a shrewd sort of geezer. This is pure conceit on my part, but it goes down well all the same when they tell me I've above average. It's after that the trouble begins, when they start probing around trying to find out what makes me tick. I don't care for this, I resent it, because if I wanted to tell them about myself I would, but

I'm not going to do it at their say-so. They're not my type, these smooth-talking clever doctors, and I could never be a friend of any of them. They don't know anything much anyway, but they've conned the Prison Commissioners into giving them a job, so good luck to them. But I'm not going to forget what they're doing is only their job, it doesn't spring from any deep-seated desire to help me.

All their questions are only questions, and they don't ever come up with answers, at least not to the patient. If I go to a doctor he'll say: 'That pain in your chest is only a touch of bronchitis, you'll be O.K. Stay in bed a few days, take these pills, you'll get over it.' But a psychiatrist, never. He says nothing, tells you nothing; doesn't let on whether you're sick or healthy, sane or insane, whether you might ever be different, or whether in the long run it'd be better if you went out and shot yourself right away.

They ask, but they don't tell. Perhaps this is because they don't know—but in that case why probe around in me? What are they hoping to come up with in the end—a recommendation I ought to be put away somewhere in a worse nick than the one I'm in?

I read once that even a good psychiatrist can get no place without co-operation from the subject he's working on. So O.K., I don't co-operate.

———

I've had it so many times, this long spiel, this 'good talking-to', all through my life. You know once in a while I get the crazy idea there must be a standard textbook with all this business in it, all these questions set out, and everybody's gone and read it up before they come and talk to me. The pattern—and the patter—is always absolutely the same, almost word for word. I know it off by heart. It goes like this:

—You know, Bob, you're an intelligent sort of person, I can tell that.

(This is always a good opening, and it's naturally very flattering, as I say. Up to here, we're getting on like a bomb.)

—And, well, look, don't take offence at this, but—well, I know it's got nothing to do with me, but I feel I must say it to you, for your own good.

(This is more than slightly fishy, and I start wanting to ask them why they're bothering then, if it's got nothing to do with them. But usually I let this one pass, and we go on. . . .)

—Now do you really think, honestly, that this keeping on going back to prison all the time is worth it?

(Of course, they don't mean 'honestly' at all. When I say honestly that I do, they can't believe I mean it.)

—But you don't want to spend all your life in prison, do you?

—No.

—Well, then . . .

—I'm not going to spend all my life in prison. I've only spent a third of it there, up to now. You said 'all'.

—All right, then, a third—do you think that's worth it?

—Yes.

—Don't you think it's a terrible waste?

—No.

—But don't you want to marry and settle down, have a home of your own and a family?

—No.

—But you might meet a nice girl whom you did want to do these things with.

—Yes, you're so right—I might. Only I haven't done yet, though I've had enough to choose from.

—But you don't want to go living with different women all the rest of your life, do you?

—Yes.

(There's usually no further argument about this one, because if they're intelligent they must know it's the only possible answer.)

—Haven't you any sense of responsibility, or desire for security?

—No.

—Don't you want to be like other people and work for your living?

—No.

(Another one no intelligent person could argue about.)

—What about when you're old, don't you want security for then?

—No.

—But isn't there anything you want to do at all?

—Oh, yes, lots of things.

—What like, what sort of things?

—Lead a life of crime for one. Stop answering your bloody silly questions for another.

You see, quite honestly, in my whole life no one's ever put a really pertinent question to me at all. All this 'Don't you think it's silly to go on like this?' stuff, it's meaningless, it's stupid; I never even have to think about the answers.

No one has ever asked me, for instance, something like— well, like: 'Which do you prefer, tea or coffee?' The answer happens to be 'coffee', and if they followed that up with: 'Why?' then I'd really have to think about the answer to that one, because I don't know why I prefer coffee to tea.

But that isn't ever what's behind their questions, usually, just the desire to know. Instead, they're all so anxious to jump in and tell me what I should do, how I should do it, what I ought to think instead of what I do think. How, if we're going to get right down to it, I really ought to want to become much more like them. Well, I don't.

It's amazing how many people there are around who think they ought to tell you, who think they know better than you what you should do. There was one only the other day: a school teacher started talking to me, telling me about how I ought to be ashamed of myself, asking me why I did things my way. So O.K., so he's a big man, what's *he* done? Spent all his life teaching a lot of kids things they don't want to know, waiting all the time for four o'clock so they can all go home, and him as glad when it comes as any of them. And yet *he* says to me: 'Why?' If he was some kind of genius himself— if he was Sir Alexander Fleming who said this to me: 'Why?'— someone, you know, who the weight of the man's intellect in his own particular field could make me respect him, well, O.K. But some schmockpot who's a bum school teacher says to me: 'Why?' I can't make it out, who's this sort of character to ask me: 'Why?' If someone does it with the interest of knowing, yes, but when someone like him gets on their high horse and starts saying to me: 'Why aren't you a good citizen?'—well, it puts my back up, that's all. And, my God, don't they get resentful about it when you start to argue with them too! Oh, no, it couldn't be their idea was wrong, it must be yours— and they get really excited and annoyed then, as soon as you cast doubt on it. You're threatening their own cherished beliefs that their way of life is the right one, all these years they've been working and saving and being good citizens . . . and then they meet you, and you don't feel ashamed of yourself or guilty or unhappy—and what's more you're not yearning to be decent and upright—and, by Christ, you *should*, according to them, and it doesn't half nark them when you're not.

And as for someone connected with the prison system itself trying to reform you, that's absolutely the end. What they're

143

trying to do is do the system a favour, not you, so that they can keep their statistics looking good and justify their existence. And if you won't fit into what they're trying to do, then it's you that's got to do the changing, not them. They treat you like a moron—which in their eyes you are.

This finding you a job business, for instance. They'll ask you if you want them to try and find you one, and as soon as you say 'How?' or 'What sort?' they come back with: 'Oh, don't worry about that, leave it to me.' In other words: 'Let me do the talking, you half-wit, leave all the brainy side to me because you're not up to it. You just do as you're told.' Any effort at thought on your part is violating their territory: if you could think, you wouldn't be there. And once more, if you argue or have the temerity to refuse something they suggest— down it goes on your card: difficult, aggressive, a thoroughly bad lot. Oh, yes, they'll help you—on condition you let them do all the deciding about what's good for you, and let them tell you how you should do it.

They make the rules for the way it's to be played, and all you must do is act like a pawn and keep in your proper position —down there. 'Take this letter, in a sealed envelope—don't on any account open it—to that address. Do exactly what the man there tells you to do—and, above all, remain polite. Don't complain, do as you're told, don't do any thinking whatsoever —and you'll be all right.' Well, no thanks.

Maybe I've met more than my share of these people, these 'helpers', these reformers. But a criminal by nature is a suspicious person, and the moment anyone starts wanting to do anything for him the first thing he wants to know is—why? What are they going to get out of it? One up for the system— that's usually it.

I've met no one, anywhere, any time, with whom it wasn't perfectly obvious, usually sooner than later, that in the end the main person he was doing it for was himself. Perhaps it was only a matter of wanting to pat his own back and being able to say to himself: 'You did a good job there, George.' But, fundamentally, that was what was always at the root of it. he was hoping for once in his life to have put a criminal straight.

Because he believed that really, in his heart, the criminal wanted to go straight, and was too stupid or too proud to admit it. And if it wasn't either of those, then he was a poor blind soul who couldn't help himself.

In my case they were wrong. They were fundamentally wrong. And that's why they all, every one of them, failed. Not one of them has ever even begun.

4

Nicked

I want to talk to you now about some of your ideas and feelings concerned with that part of your life— a considerable part—which you've spent involved with the machinery of authority. . . .

I

The Police

When you're arrested, what are your reactions at that moment?

I think the first thing's annoyance—with myself. How could I be so stupid as to get nicked? What's gone wrong, what have I forgotten, where have I made the mistake? That passes off gradually, then I calm down and start trying to think how I'm going to get out of the situation.

By resorting to violence to get away, do you mean?

Oh, no, not necessarily—there's no point to that unless the stakes are very high. I mean more along the lines of: 'Are they going to be able to make this stick, can I talk myself out of it, what can I think of that they've overlooked?'

Naturally you don't like it when the police have got you, but there's not a great deal of resentment, really. After all, it's their job, catching criminals—though sometimes they get over-enthusiastic and try to pin things on you which you haven't done. They're not fussy about stretching the evidence to make it fit, particularly if they've got a lot of unsolved cases on their books which they're trying to clear up. And that you do resent, of course.

What sort of a relationship is there between the police and criminals?

On the whole I'd think you could best describe it as a working relationship. With the experienced police, that is.

A lot of the young ones start off by wanting to be heroes and win themselves medals for catching criminals, but as they grow up that attitude drops away; they settle down into doing something which is just a job like anything else.

With the police you've usually got a relationship which is based on mutual recognition of certain facts—number one, it's a criminal's way of life to go thieving, and number two, it's the policeman's job to try and catch him for it. This gives you a basic approach to each other, in fact the police are the only people apart from other criminals who accept you for what you are. They don't try to reform you. This makes things a good deal simpler all round: you know where you are with them, and they know where they are with you.

Naturally if you're stupid about things, leave clues all over the place—bits of torn-off clothing, blood-stained fingerprints, and so on—well, the cozzpots'll get you and you deserve it. They're not all idiots, and if you make it plain as daylight some particular job was done by you they'll nick you for it.

But in the majority of cases they've only got hunches to go on. Any job, by the way it was done, who was around at the time, who's looking prosperous soon afterwards—they've got a pretty shrewd idea who did it. If the pressure's on them from up above they'll go all out to fasten it on you, especially if there's no way they can make a bit out of it for themselves.

Incidentally, the best description I've come across yet of this relationship is in *The Loneliness of the Long Distance Runner* by Alan Sillitoe. That's a marvellous book. I suppose at one time or another I must have read most things written on the subject of crime and criminals, because I've got an interest in it and I consider I know a bit about it. This book isn't merely the best I've read, it's so far ahead of all the others it's in a class of its own. Sillitoe has got a terrific grasp of the workings of a criminal mind. I can't imagine how, unless he's been inside himself. To me, he sounds as though he must have done a lot of bird, and I mean that as a compliment. He gets over the relationship exactly in that book.

Can we get back to these thoughts of yours about trying to get out of the situation when you're arrested? How can you do that, for instance, if you've been caught red-handed?

Well, of course, you can't. Obviously they're going to make it stick. So you have to start thinking of ways round it.

What 'ways round it' can there be when it's like that?

The only one I know of is the usual one, to bung them.

What does that mean?

Pay them money, bribe them.

Bribe the police?

Sure. But what do you look so surprised about—don't you read the papers?

Yes, but those are only occasional cases, surely?

The ones you read about are only occasional. I've bought my way out of more charges than I've done time for.

Let's get this quite clear—are you saying that bribing the police is a regular occurrence?

I should have thought this was well known. You remember the Brighton case a year or two back? I was in the nick the whole time that was on, and everybody was talking about it all day long, naturally. In all the expressions of opinion and comments about it, the only thing I never once heard was anyone say they were surprised. Everybody knows about this, everybody who's had anything to do with the police—it's as common as London Transport buses or dogs or any other part of the daily scene.

Tell me some more about this. How does it work?

Well, I must make it clear at the start I'm talking only about the plain-clothes mob, the C.I.D.; not the uniformed police. Most of them are beginners who don't count for much, so it's a waste of time and money trying to bung them.

And if you're going in for bunging, by the way, it's got to

151

be kept straight. Trying to be clever about it will only get you trouble. A friend of mine called Stamper found that out. He was taken in for something and agreed to bung the Law, and made arrangements with a C.I.D. sergeant to meet him a couple of nights later in a pub.

Being a bit vindictive by nature, Stamper thought he'd be clever and he phoned the rubber-heel mob at Scotland Yard. They're the ones who do the investigating into the police force itself. He told them how he was due to meet this sergeant and hand over a couple of hundred quid—time, place, everything. But when Stamper arrived at the pub to keep his appointment there wasn't a cozzpot in sight except two from the rubber-heel mob. Of course the sergeant never turned up because one of the Scotland Yard blokes had tipped him off, most of them having taken the bung themselves often enough in their time.

And that wasn't the end of it. A few days later Stamper was getting into his van near Blackfriars when two C.I.D. men came up and nicked him. 'What's this for?' says Stamper, all outrage and innocence. 'You've got nothing on me.'

'Oh, no?' says one of the C.I.D. men. 'Well, what about those rolls of cloth in the back of your van? They're off a warehouse job in Stepney last night.' And there they were in the back of Stamper's van. He got twelve months for it and a lesson.

But if you play it straight you'll usually be O.K. What happens probably goes something like this: You get caught for something and taken down to the station by the uniform mob. When you get there you say nothing until the C.I.D. arrive. They turn up to make 'inquiries' about the job you were caught for and possibly a few others they're trying to clear up at the same time. After a while two of them take you into an office for questioning. Probably they'll offer you a cup of tea to start the ball rolling. It's all got to be played according to the rules, so you pretend you're strangers. Of course they've nicked you before, so you're not. The big one, the senior of the two, makes the start.

—Got much form, son?

—Yes, a bit. Six previous.

(He whistles and shakes his head sadly.)

—Mm, that's not so good, is it, son? So what do you reckon you'll get for this?

—Three years maybe. Perhaps a bit less, perhaps a bit more.

—Yes, I'm afraid you will get three for this, son, at the very least. Wouldn't you think he'd get three, George?

(The other one nods, looking very worried about it.)

—Yes, I would. They're a bit naughty at the Sessions just now.

(We all look depressed, all three of us. The big one gets almost fatherly.)

—Three years is a lot for a boy of your age, son. It's going to be tough for you.

(This is where it's all nicely lined up: this is where you can lead into it.)

—Well, can't we do something about it?

—It's a bit late for that now, son, I'm afraid. You should have thought about this before you did it, shouldn't you?

—Yes, but I didn't. So O.K., what can we do?

—No, son, we can't do anything like that, really we can't, can we, George?

(George can always be relied on: he knows the stooge's part backwards.)

—No, things are very dodgy just now. The higher-ups are getting a bit naughty lately, we've had too many cases we couldn't make stick.

(More head-shaking all round—but of course you carry on.)

—Well, there's no taste in nothing, is there? Are you going to be satisfied with all the glory and no money?

—We'd like to help you, son, it's not that, but as George says, the higher-ups are——

153

—Sure, sure, I know all that. But how much?

—Well, I'm very doubtful about it, son . . . it'd be a question of how much you could go to, really. And even then I'm not saying we'll be able to do anything.

—Fifty.

—Good God, no, that's out of the question, son. Why, the Guv'nor himself'd want a one-er for his whack alone.

—All right then, give us a price.

—It'd have to be two-fifty, son, two-fifty at the very least.

—Balls. I could get Rose Heilbron for that and fight you.

—Even Rosie Heilbron couldn't get you off with less than three, boy, not with what we've got on you. Look, I'll tell you what we'll do—we'll do you a favour. A one-er for the Guv'nor, and fifty each for me and George here, that's cut price. Two hundred all told, how's that?

(It's not much use arguing about it, because you know this is about the best you're going to get, so you've got to put up with it.)

—O.K., I'll do my best. But you'll have to give me bail so I can go and make it.

—When can you make it for, son?

—Friday. Thursday night, perhaps.

—We're taking a risk, you know that?

—So am I. I might get nicked while I'm out making it.

—No, now don't do that, son, or we'll all be in the cart. You meet George here in the Waggon on Thursday night, but remember—let him do the approach, don't you speak to him until he comes over and speaks to you.

So you've got yourself bail, and until Thursday night to do a job and earn the money. What often happens is that when Thursday comes you can only raise half of it, because you've picked a job in a hurry and it didn't turn out as good as you'd hoped. The cozzpots are usually decent about it, but you have to make sure they've got the full amount before your case comes up in court, otherwise they'll leave you to it.

If you've given them the bung, when you go to court for your case you say to your counsel: 'I think the Law's not very strong on a couple of points,' and he knows what you mean—that you've bunged them and if he presses he'll find a get-out for you.

The prosecuting counsel can soon sense when the Law have been bunged too, because suddenly all the stuffing goes out of the case. The detective giving evidence will say something like: 'When I arrested him, he said I'd made a terrible mistake,' instead of their usual: 'He said: "It's a fair cop, guv." ' Or he'll drop a hint they're not 100 per cent certain they've got the right man. Sometimes if there's no other way out they'll make a deliberate mistake, something like: 'I had a pretty good idea he'd done it because I arrested him once before for a job he was caught red-handed on.' If he lets out you've got previous convictions like this, the judge has got no alternative but to dismiss you, because they can't say about those things until you've been found guilty. They have all sorts of variations, but once they've taken the bung you can rely on it some way or another you'll be safe and dry.

(A similar allegation of police acceptance of bribes can be found in *Miscarriages of Justice* by C. G. L. Du Cann, Barrister-at-Law. Muller, 1960. T.P.)

2

A Screwsman

You once said you found criminals much more interesting to be with than straight people. Of those you've known, who was the most outstanding, not as a criminal but as a person?

It's difficult to pick out one from so many who were memorable . . . but I think one of the most unusual was a bloke whose name was Billy Shakespeare. I originally met him in the nick, but later I knew him outside too—and he was probably the best screwsman I've ever met in my life. I've known him slide a five-hundredweight safe down four flights of stairs in a block of flats, entirely on his own, without making a sound or even getting out of breath. This was all the more remarkable because he weighed fifteen stone and looked as fat and out of condition as a pig. Another astonishing thing about him was that, on a job, he never spoke a single word from start to finish; but off it he never stopped talking from morning till night.

As I say, I first ran into him in prison where we were both in the mail-bag shop. The other striking thing besides his size was the fantastic ugliness of the man. One of his eyes had a violent cast in it, his nose had been broken and never put straight and spread almost from one ear to the other, his cheeks were so scarred and marked it looked as though a razor mob had used him for a strop, and his teeth were broken and blackened. Yet to hear him talk about women he was Errol Flynn and Casanova rolled into one, and if only a hundredth part of what he said was true there must still have been plenty who found him attractive.

His talk matched his general appearance—it was huge and unlikely. But the fantastic thing about him was that despite yourself you were carried away to such an extent you really believed all he was saying. As a talker he could have given Oscar Wilde points and still beaten him hands down, and as a dreamer Walter Mitty wasn't in it. Prisoners are not the easiest of audiences, most of them are unsympathetic and unbelieving even when someone's speaking the truth. Yet the way Billy told his tales it was impossible not to go along with him. It was only later when you started to think about them you realized they must be rubbish. But he never told them for any purpose, there was nothing he got out of them except the sheer enjoyment of talking.

Whatever subject cropped up in conversation, Billy always knew all about it only better. I happened to mention to him one day I'd been reading Sassoon's book, *Memoirs of a Fox-hunting Man*, and that was as far as I got. 'It's all rubbish,' says Billy. 'The bloke's got no idea what he's talking about. Fox hunting? He's never been on a horse in his life. I used to belong to the Pytchley Hunt myself and I remember once . . .' And I was spellbound.

Any name that was mentioned, it didn't matter who it was, Shakespeare had met him—and, what's more, had usually had to put him in his place. I think it was the first day I met him in the workshop some character remarked he'd written to Viscount Southwood asking him to take up his case in the *People*, and Billy was away like a streak. . . .

'Southwood? Yes, he's a good feller, he'll help you if anybody can. Used to know him myself before the war, what was he called—Elias, Jacob Elias, that's who he was in those days, yes, a very nice feller. Came into my office one day—I was working with a colleague of his, bloke called Martin, we were running a chain of hotels. Think he was toying with the idea of going into the hotel business himself, though nothing came of it. I remember this day particularly, because it was raining and he'd got no mac and was drenched, and I thought it was funny he should be out walking in the rain instead of being driven around by a chauffeur—but he was like that was Elias, no side to him at all, a very nice bloke. And he said to me —I can still see him standing there, wiping the rain off his collar with a silk handkerchief—he said: "Billy, I know you're a shrewd man and this has got nothing to do with me—but I should keep an eye on that co-director of yours if I were you. That Martin, he'd ponce on his grandmother if he thought it would get him ten bob." He meant well by it, I knew that, and I thought how nice it was of him to pass on the friendly tip.'

Up to there it sounded, if not likely, at least not absolutely out of the question. It just could have happened—apart from the language, which his listeners were too ignorant to know any better about. Elias was a nice bloke, O.K. Having got you into this sort of bemused state, Billy ran on:

'Yet you know for all his cleverness—and he was clever, was Elias, there was no doubt about that—he hadn't got Martin summed up right. Because in actual fact Martin was a real, soft-hearted kid when it came to business and anyone could pull the wool over his eyes. That was just what all the managers of these hotels we were running were doing, every one of them, rooking us right, left, and centre. Eventually it got to such a state we had to clear 'em out, the whole lot of 'em, seventeen there were in those days. The company had my name— Shakespeare Hotels—you still see a few of them up and down the country, they've still kept the name.'

By now everyone was nodding their heads—yes, they'd seen a Shakespeare hotel somewhere.

'The biggest villain of all was one up in Scotland, naturally, because he was farthest away from head office. What he was getting away with—well, you wouldn't believe me if I told you, so I won't. We didn't find out how bad it was until we got this complaint from Lord—oh, what was his name, Strabolgi, was it? No, that was something else; Lord—Lord—Nicholas, Nichols, that's it, Lord Nichols—who'd been staying at this place and wrote complaining he was charged forty-five bob for two chicken sandwiches and a whisky-and-soda. Forty-five bob, I ask you! That was a lot more money in those days than it is now, remember! So there was nothing else for it but I had to go up there and sort this manager out.

'Got off the train at Aberdeen, I remember, and then had to take a taxi out to this place, miles out of town it was, cost me over five quid just for the fare. When I got out there was some slag on the door, all gold braid and nose in the air, wouldn't let me in! Didn't think I looked good enough for the tone of the place, though God knows why.'

He was dead serious when he said this, and those who were listening looked at each other and winked. It was obvious from his facial appearance why the commissionaire tried to stop him, but of course Billy couldn't understand that. (By the time you were thinking like this, you were lost. You were so far in with the story you were working parts of it out for yourself instead of standing back and doubting it.)

'So, anyway, I give this creep a shove in the chest that nearly knocked him off the portico, and in I went. Up comes the manager screaming and yelling about who did I think I was barging into his place like this—so I just looked at him, and I said: "Back in your office, mug—I'm Shakespeare." He looked as though somebody'd cut him off at the knees with a scythe. He started to tremble like a jelly. From then on it was: "Oh, yes, Mr Shakespeare, this way, sir, do sit down, Mr Shakespeare, you'd like a drink, wouldn't you—whisky, yes, certainly, sir; here, have the whole bottle." So I sat down on his desk—not on a chair, mark you, but on the actual desk, right in the middle of all his papers and things with my arse—a bit of psychology, see. And then I said: "Right. Fetch that rat in off the door for a start."

'So in they brought him. Of course they'd told him who I was. Honestly, I've never seen anything like this, I never thought it could happen except in some tripy book. He went down there and then on the carpet on his hands and knees, and he caught hold of my shoes and he said: "Oh, Mr Shakespeare, sir, please forgive me, I didn't know it was you, sir. I've got a wife and three children, sir, please don't give me the sack, Mr Shakespeare." I can't tell you how irritating it was, I can't bear people touching my feet, you know, and he was damn' near pulling me off the desk. So I said to him: "Stop that. Stand up, you rat!" Well, when he got up I took my chiv out of my hip pocket and I held it right under his nose, and I said: "You bleeding mug, I've a good mind to stripe you—and then you!" And I whipped round and nearly cut the manager's head off, swishing the chiv just past his ear. You should have seen them both—they thought they were in for a real carving.'

Billy laughed at the memory of it . . . and then he stopped and quietly got on with his work. Naturally everybody started: 'But what happened, Billy? Did you give the bloke the sack or what?'

He shrugged. 'Well, what could I have done? After all, it was true he'd got a wife and three kids. You can't throw someone out like that. No, I let him stay on. Not the manager, of course, he had to go. But the other one stayed—used to send me a Christmas card every year without fail, right up to when the war broke out.'

That was the way it went, and at the end of it everyone would think what a decent bloke at heart Billy was, not sacking the doorman like that. . . . It'd be hours before you started pondering the whole thing and coming to the conclusion it had all been made up on the spur of the moment.

One day on exercise I was walking round with a mug who suddenly said: 'Heh, you know that Billy Shakespeare, he's a real nice bloke, he's going to give me a job when I get out. He's got a business up in Birmingham, apparently, making those coloured saucepans and things, you know, you see them advertised in the papers a lot. He's a director of it or something, wants me to act as a driver for him because his leg's bad where he got caught by that bomb-fragment in Tobruk. Says I won't have to wear a uniform, none of that "Sir" business, nothing like that. I can use his car myself at week-ends, if I want. My keep, all found, plus five quid a week for pocket money. Only one condition—I've got to keep off the booze. Well, I reckon it's a chance and I'd be a mug not to take it, what do you think?'

'Sure,' I said, 'it sounds marvellous. When are you due out?'

'Next April,' he says. 'Why?'

'Oh, I was just wondering,' I said. 'Shakespeare's not coming out himself till four years next June.'

I don't think it'd even crossed Billy's mind he was conning this mug. He'd started talking and that was where it led to. To talk was a sort of illness he'd got, and he couldn't help it: whatever the subject or the person mentioned, he had to go. It was: 'Yes, I remember Lord Rosebery saying to me in the Jockey Club tent,' or: 'You mugs won't know this, but Hitler himself was over in this country in 1934, staying for a week-end as a guest of the Mitfords. Nice bloke, had a few minutes' chat with him myself, and he said: "Billy," he said, "I can tell you're a straight man and I want you to know . . ." ' About the only thing I never heard Billy claim—which can only have been because he hadn't yet thought of it—was Sir Lionel Fox had asked him to reorganize the whole prison system.

To listen to him did more to pass the time in prison than anything ever invented. It was fantastic, it was incredible, and yet you couldn't help believing it because of the reasonableness and conviction with which he talked. But I shall always remember, best of all, one particular story he came out with one day in the workshop to a group of those sitting near him, that he must somehow, because of its ending, have worked out in his mind beforehand. Perhaps he'd done that and then stored it away until the opportunity for telling it arose. But whether he had or not, on this particular day he excelled himself.

It was at a time when the King was ill, and the newspapers were full of reports about his doctors going in and out of the Palace attending him. Some bloke had a newspaper and he was reading out a list of these doctors' names. I forget the real name of the man, but whoever it was, Sir Somebody-Somebody, as soon as he heard it Billy let out a low whistle and shook his head in amazement.

'My good God,' he said slowly, 'how that feller's got on all right. A "Sir" is he, now?—well, well. You know, I remember him when he was just a kid, starting out on his career. His first job was on a ship, the S.S. *Parradine* it was—one of the old Middlesbrough and Hartlepools line, cargo and passengers, doing the Hook–Oslo–Bergen–Archangel run. Joined us the first week after he'd qualified, remember him coming aboard—fine, upstanding young feller, very good looking, blue eyes, fair hair, kit-bag over his shoulder, and all that. Said to me: "Excuse me, sir"—very polite he was—"excuse me, sir, I wonder if you could tell me where the captain is?" Don't know who he thought I was, must have been the uniform that did it, I suppose. I was only the purser, after all, but of course he was real green, just out of college. Well, I don't think any young man can have had a more upsetting maiden trip. Sick as a dog he was for the first two days, and then on the third day I suddenly get this terrific pain in my right side. Couldn't stand up, cold sweat pouring off me, grey face, all the rest of it. Course I knew what it was, seen it often myself when I was doing my four years at Guy's. Tried to keep going, but it was no use. Collapsed. So along comes this young chap to have a look at me. I don't know which of us was the greyer, me with the pain or him with knowing what it meant.

' "What do you think, Billy?" he says to me after he'd had a look at me.

' "Well," I says, "you know what it is, don't you, son? And you know there's only one thing you can do."

' "Yes, Billy," he says. "You're quite right, but I'm not very happy about it. I don't like appendicectomy." (That's the trade name for appendix operations in case any of you ignorant mugs don't know.) "And what's more," he says, "to tell you the honest truth I've never done one, Billy, and that's a fact."

'He was in such a state I was more sorry for him than I was for myself—after all, a young lad, first job, down with the sea-sickness and then this—it was enough to finish his career before he'd even started, if he made a mess of it.

'So I said to him: "Look, son," I said, "can you fix me up with a good spinal anaesthetic—can you manage that all right?" Yes, he said, he thought he could. "O.K.," I said, "now don't you worry, son. There's a big mirror in the captain's cabin, isn't there? Well, we'll rig that up over the table for a start."

'So that's what we did. I lay on the table, and with this mirror I could watch him every step of the way and tell him what to do. He was as scared as hell, but he was a good lad and took it nice and slowly, stopping every few minutes so I could check it for him. Took a long time, of course, doing it like that—nearly two hours all told before we'd finished. He was a very neat careful worker, though. Did a first-class job.'

Billy rose to his feet and slowly pulled aside his shirt. 'You take a good look—you can't even see the scar now.'

A Prison Governor

And who from the side of authority made most impression on you in prison?

I don't know that he made much impression on me personally, but there is one person who to me represents in essence, you might say, all the authoritarian aspects of prison. He's a governor—or he was—and I've been in one of his prisons on two occasions.

You couldn't really imagine him living anywhere else, he almost gave you the feeling he must have been born in a prison, in a place of blocks of granite, cold and hard, where men shouted and ordered you about and the only feelings were hatred or indifference. I suppose at some time in his life somebody must have loved him, his mother perhaps, but she must have been the only one. Certainly all the people I ever came across in prison loathed and feared him—and that included not only the prisoners but the screws as well. Even now, you still only need to mention his name to anyone who's been under him and it brings a scowl. His name was a very well known one in the prison world.

He wasn't very big in build, except for his face which always seemed a size too large for the rest of him somehow. It looked as though it had been cut out of the same stone they'd used to make the walls, all sharp edges and steep angles. When he was younger he'd had some kind of accident which had left him with a permanent limp, a sort of shuffle that made his body flop about when he walked, like it wanted to go in a different direction. Yet his head didn't move like that, it was always absolutely steady as though it floated along on its own. There was a common rumour this disability had been the result of him being attacked once by a prisoner, but I don't think it was true, it was something he'd had most of his life.

He had been attacked by prisoners, more than once, that was certainly true. One time it happened when I was doing bird, some bloke got at him, knocked him down and kicked him before the screws dragged him off. It must have bruised him, and if that happened to a screw the screw would go off sick—but not this character. Within a couple of hours he was doing a tour of the prison, his face fastened up with sticking-plaster, just so everyone could see him on his feet. It was sheer bravado because he'd already done his official round for the day. 'Take a good look at me, you bastards, I'm still here.'

Unlike most prison governors you get these days, he was one of the old school who'd come up through the ranks—ordinary prison officer, principal officer, chief, deputy governor, the lot. By the time he'd done all that there was nothing he didn't know when he got to the top. Whatever excuse a man could offer for being in trouble in the nick, he'd heard it all before—in fact he was there when that particular excuse was first thought up. As a result he never accepted any excuses, never even bothered to listen to them. If you were up on a charge in front of him, you knew it wasn't worth making the effort: so you didn't try. As far as he was concerned, when one of his screws charged you, that was sufficient—you'd done it.

He was supposed to be the original of the old story about the governor a prisoner complained to, about him always taking the screw's word and never listening to prisoners. His reply was: 'If one of my officers reported you'd been riding round the landing on a motor-bike, I'd want to know where you got the petrol from.'

When you did come up in front of him on a charge, it was all over in about thirty seconds flat. The screw said what you were supposed to have done, and you shook your head when you were asked if you'd anything to say. Then he said: 'Three, three, and three'—and you were shot out again. It was always the same: three days bread-and-water, three days loss of remission, three days loss of privileges. No question of being let off with a warning, being asked why you'd done it, nothing like that. You weren't a human being, you were a piece of mechanism in his machine that needed oiling. And the only lubricant he used was 'Three, three, and three'.

The screws were as frightened of him as the prisoners, because he'd put them on a charge soon as look at them, if he caught them not doing their job properly. And their job, as he saw it, was to keep shouting at the cons. You might be working one day, perhaps a small group of you cementing some brickwork with one screw to look after you and everybody taking it easy. Then suddenly the screw would start raving and swearing at you: 'Get a move on there, you lazy bastards, come along, come along, *come along*!' You knew what it meant: next minute the governor was going to appear round the corner.

He had a trick of standing on the centre, moving his head slowly from side to side, seeing everything that was going on. How he did it I'll never know, but you could be miles away from him, three floors up and eighteen cells along, talking out of the corner of your mouth to the bloke in the next cell while you were both standing at your doors waiting to go to classes— and suddenly this yell would come up from him down on the centre—'A4/56, stop that talking!' It was a mystery how he did it.

Yet it was a funny thing . . . you couldn't help feeling a kind of sneaking respect for him. At least one thing with him was you always knew where you stood. With a lot of these new-type governors, you don't. A bloke'll put down to see him to ask for a special visit, and he'll refuse it. The next day he'll be walking round the prison polite and smiling, 'Good morning, good morning' all over the place. The bloke resents it because it looks as though he's only friendly when it doesn't mean anything. A governor who decides between one man and another, each case on its merits, who shall have a favour and who not, all he does is create bad feeling.

This one—there was never any doubt about who he liked or didn't like: he didn't like anybody. It was no use asking him for favours, he wouldn't give them. No use expecting consideration, he didn't use it. No use hoping for mercy, he'd never heard of it. And you knew he didn't give these things to anybody else either—not even to his own screws if they fell down on the job. He handed out terror all round, so at least he was fair.

He was a pig-headed authoritarian without frills, who'd snarled his way up to the top without giving favours to anyone. He brought no fancy ideas of reform into prison that nobody understood—but at least he gave everyone a feeling of solidarity, of having something in common. They all hated *him*.

4

Penal Reform

And prison itself—what's it like?

· At times I've rather savoured the details of prison, I must admit—the funny bits, the cruel bits, the kindness one sometimes meets . . . even occasionally from screws. You know, if a screw's kind sometimes, it seems to have much more value than other people's kindness.

But what's prison like? There's no excuse for people not knowing nowadays. So many books on the subject by the people who've been there, a lot of them very good. I can't think one more description would say anything new. I'm not recommending it as a place, of course—from beginning to end it's a waste of time, something that's got to be passed through with as little mental damage as possible. You won't come out better than you went in, and you could easily be worse: duller, less ambitious, less alive. It has no value for most people who do time—which is a pity, because I'd guess myself that about 70 per cent of the material in prisons was salvageable if only somebody went about it the right way.

Such as? What should they do?

Are you asking me to make suggestions for penal reform?

Why not? You've had plenty of experience of it.

Well, O.K., I suppose I could try. The one thing you do have in prison is plenty of time to think—and this is one of the things I've occasionally passed the time with—what I would do if it was me running the place.

To start with, I don't believe all prisons should be open or anything like that. If they were I for one would leave immediately, so would plenty of others. Open prisons are all right for first offenders, but for people like me you've obviously got to have closed ones. But I can't see any reason why, once you've made the security effective, they can't do something better with the insides. By this I don't mean paint them in pastel shades, wireless in every cell, window-boxes, and so on. I mean something of practical use. I don't mean reformative schemes full of humaneness and enlightenment either, which is what all the emphasis is on these days.

To me, this whole idea of trying to reform people's character by friendliness is rubbish. The grandly titled 'Norwich Experiment', for instance, where the screws are encouraged to act as friends and counsellors—it's complete balls. The men don't want to be friends with the screws any more than the screws want to be with the men. All the money spent on training prison personnel along these lines is money poured down a drain. For the simple reason that the whole scheme is based on talk, on good advice—which prisoners don't want, don't understand, and, a lot of them, heartily resent. They've been having it all their lives ever since they were kids whenever they were in trouble. If they could pay any attention to it, if they were the sort of people who could benefit from good advice, they wouldn't be in prison in the first place. On top of that, it's impossible for jailors to sit on both sides of the fence. When they try, it simply leads to confusion in their own minds and everyone else's. Whatever a screw says to a prisoner, there's always bound to be the feeling of an order behind it. How can screws reform men's characters like that? Most men in prison, they're way beyond the help of top-class psychiatrists, let alone dim-witted screws.

Talk has no value at all. It's telling a man what to think, instead of letting him think for himself. But unless he does think for himself rehabilitation is impossible. He's got to learn to do things at his own direction, because he wants to— not at someone else's say-so.

What can he think in prison, what does he do there which teaches him to think? Sew mail-bags? Pick coir? Break up surplus post-office equipment? These are activities for morons, requiring no mental effort of any kind. Any sign of thought will be put a stop to at once because it's certain to be breaking the regulations. The pressure all the time is not on thought, but on obeying orders, doing as you're told, not causing trouble.

I think they should take this pressure off, give up all their schemes of trying to convert people to goodness by talk, and substitute something far more important: self-help. Teach a man how to help himself by doing something constructive and useful that he can earn his living with when he goes out. They make an attempt at it now with C.T., but it's nothing like good enough, and could be extended in all directions. The majority, all they ever get taught is mail-bag sewing or brush-making. Can you make a living at those things when you go out? Are they any use to anyone in the world?

They could start in all prison workshops, not as now where men pass the time wasting it, but where men are doing a proper trade. Panel-beating, paint-spraying, machining, lathe work, milling—anything you like, so long as it bears some relation to the sort of work people do outside, so a man can try to get that sort of job when he goes out. In a garage, for instance: if a man had learned something about automobile engineering while he was inside, not from a book he'd got himself out of the library but from actual working in a repair shop in the prison—well, at least when he went out he might stand some chance of getting a job.

Who'd train them? Well, when you think of the material

there is in prison, men already there who worked at trades outside, you get some idea of the waste at present. Not long ago there was a case, a fitter-welder who got a long sentence. He could at least pay off some of his so-called 'debt to the community' by teaching what he knows to other men while he's inside. But of course he'll be put to sewing mail-bags.

This whole thing would mean, naturally, that prisoners would have to take much more part in the running of the prison themselves, and this itself might even do them some good. Other prisoners would certainly be more willing to learn from a skilled man, one of their own number, than they are at present from instructor-screws, most of whom are poor because the job's poorly paid and doesn't attract good men.

Or take another example. The number of men in prison who know something about radio engineering must be pretty big. They could be doing something useful if they were teaching others. But all they ever get a chance to use their skill on at present is making contraband miniature wirelesses to exchange for tobacco.

It wouldn't cost an inordinate sum to equip a prison with proper training workshops, and the initial expenses would soon be covered by what the men working in them turned out. One thing there's no shortage of in prisons is manpower, and these places could be self-supporting: that should be the aim. They've got a few already, I know: but they are only a few, and there's no great imaginative new scheme in the air for extension at all. The usual cry is: 'No money, we can't afford it.' But a government which finds millions for guided missiles and hydrogen bombs could find the money for this O.K. if it wanted to—and know it was being spent on something a bit more constructive than blowing half the world's population to pieces.

The whole point is that with this training at the back of him a man on discharge wouldn't need the pathetic attempts of the after-care services to help him either. They're always complaining about the difficulties of finding work for a man who's got a criminal record and is unskilled as well—so this would solve a large part of their problem too. How can they be expected to find jobs for men who aren't on a par with others? But if a man's got a skill he can earn with, well, surely that's better than giving him a pound, a letter to a flop-house, and a few words of good advice. Trained, he's under obligation to nobody, and feels he's got a chance of making a go of things outside.

Those who don't want to learn in prison, O.K., they can sweep up the machine-shop floor. But put the opportunity there for those who do. I think this would work, this idea: I think it's worth at least a try.

Keep the screws for security, of course, to maintain order and stop people running away: that's what they like doing, and what they do best. But that should be their only purpose. The rest should be left to the inmates.

5

Free

And the other side of your life, the part you spend out of the shadow—let's talk now about some aspects of this. . . .

A Bird

You know up to now one thing we've hardly discussed at all is the position of women in your life—obviously they've figured fairly prominently, but you've said very little about them. Has there ever been one who meant more than all the others?

No—not until recently anyway. But I think the girl who's with me now does. Maybe I'm getting old.

Can you think of one from all those before who was particularly remarkable or unusual?

All women are remarkable, all women are unusual. The odd thing is, most of the women I've known have all been good to me however much of a bastard I was to them. They've been affectionate and loyal—and that's always been the most important thing to me about women, loyalty.

Fidelity sexually, do you mean?

No. That's important, sure: but I mean more in the sense of standing by you, not running you down to other people, standing up for you when you're being criticized or got at— that sort of loyalty. Sex itself can be well over-rated—especially when you haven't got it, then it becomes paramount. But on the whole I've done well, I've been lucky, I've had tremendous enjoyment from women. When you ask me to recall one . . . the field's pretty wide, but perhaps a bird called Katie Spencer was one of the most unusual. Not because she meant more to me than many others: she didn't. Nor because she was any better in bed—she was good enough, but she wasn't sensational. I'll choose her because of the startling first impression she made.

I met her one night in a club in Bayswater. I suppose that word 'club' suggests all sorts of things to people—romantic dens of vice, haunts of bohemians, wildness, glamour, excitement. You hear blokes in prison talking about the marvellous times they've had in 'West End clubs'. Whenever they have one in a film—which they always do if they can possibly drag it in—the impression's always that these are marvellous places.

In actual fact, they're dull and pointless. They exist for one reason only—to make money for the people running them. A room in an old basement, a carpet, red plush seats round the walls, a couple of coffee tables, a bar made out of plywood in one corner, a bloke playing a piano in the other—and you're in business, you've got yourself a club. Get a licence to remain open from three in the afternoon till eleven at night, stick a mug on the door to let in 'members' only, and that's it. Naturally, at closing time, you throw out the unknowns and shut the door—the proprietor describes this as 'getting rid of the mugs' —and then the rest stay on to drink or gamble or smoke charge. In actual fact, the ones who stay are the mugs.

The people who frequent these places are usually the sort whose only interest in life is drinking. They like to do it without interruption in a place where nobody minds what they look like or talk about. Two boys, for instance: they might want to have a drink and a dance together. They couldn't do it in an ordinary pub, not if they wanted to put their arms round each other. But in a club there's nothing queer about queers. Or a brass might want a break for an hour or two. If she goes to a pub it'll look as though she's there on business; in a club she can have a quiet drink on her own and no one'll bother her.

That was how I met this bird Katie Spencer—she was a

178

brass in off the Bayswater Road for a break, having a drink with two others who were also having a rest. One of them was someone I knew, a girl called Rita: she called me over to join them.

I used to live with Rita for a few weeks. While we were doing it I wouldn't let her go out on the turf, because of this thing I've got about not poncing—and after a while she started telling the other two about it, pulling my leg. No malice in it, nothing unpleasant: she and her friend were laughing about it. But Katie wasn't. She was just sitting there saying nothing, watching me out of those marvellous, big green eyes she had, sipping her drink and smoking her cigarette. She had long auburn hair, very thin delicate wrists and hands, long legs— quite a dish. Her expression was enigmatic: for all I knew she was probably thinking I was some kind of idiot. If so, she must have been a good judge of character.

Anyway, after a while these other two birds decide to blow and get back on the job. Katie still hadn't said anything, not a word, but she stayed sitting there and let them go. Even then she kept silent for a while, just sat and looked at me, drawing slowly on her cigarette. When she did eventually speak, you couldn't say she went round and round the point exactly. She said: 'Like to come case with me?'

'No, thanks,' I said. 'Nothing personal, of course.'

She blew the cigarette smoke out of the corner of her mouth. 'Got a girl?'

'No,' I said. 'Not a girl, no. Several—all different.'

She pushed her empty glass towards me. 'You'd like to buy me another drink.' No question: just a statement.

I'm always a pushover, so I did; then we had one or two more. The conversation was quite aimless, like you always have in these places—Did you ever know so-and-so? Yes I did. What's happened to him now? I don't know, but I met some-one who told me . . . That sort of thing.

Then, while she was lighting another cigarette, she came back to it again. 'Why don't you want to come case with me?'

She'd got good reason for asking, I suppose. She was an attractive girl, and looked as though she usually got what she wanted. I don't even know why myself, unless it's because I like to do the chasing and the conquest is the real attraction. I gave a vague shrug.

'You'd enjoy it,' she said. 'I'll promise you that.'

'Yes, maybe I would,' I said. 'But it doesn't appeal much, I'm beginning to feel I've had it all.'

'All?'

She stretched out her hand towards me across the table, keeping her eyes fixed on my face. Then, very slowly and methodically, she stubbed out her cigarette on the back of her hand.

I nearly ran up the wall; I could feel my hair shoot up on the back of my neck. Of all the pains I'm scared of, burning's the worst. I only need to touch the tip of my finger with a match and I'm screaming round everyone I know about it for weeks. Despite what I said earlier she was a bad judge of character, because that sadism lark to me is right out.

I don't know if she'd expected my eyes to light up with desire or what. What did happen is I must have gone pale green because she offered to buy me a drink, then she said she was sorry she'd upset me, but there was nothing else she could think of that might appeal. I said nice, ordinary, straightforward, non-perverted stuff suited me best, thank you, and she'd probably turned my stomach now for weeks. She got very contrite about this and insisted on coming home with me.

So there it was, and she moved into my place for a while. What she was worrying about with all that sadistic stuff to get me excited, with a body like she'd got, I just don't know. Apart from the fact she was keen for me to bite lumps out of her and I was never hungry enough, we got on very well. Of course, after a few days we had the usual argument about her not seeing any reason why she couldn't go out on the turf to get us a few luxuries, but I wouldn't have it, and she had to lead the life of a lady of leisure. Or at least she had to lead a life of leisure, let's put it like that.

This meant that after a while she was short of things to do to pass the time, so she took to reading. Being of an inventive turn of mind, whatever she came across in a book, she tried it. One time she read paraffin would kill woodworm in furniture. We didn't have woodworm, but she painted the chairs with paraffin all the same, just to be on the safe side. The place stank.

All this was apt to make life a bit difficult. It was bad enough while she only read household hints, but when she got on to fiction then the trouble really started. Whoever the main character was in the book, Katie was it. Tess of the D'Urbevilles was a grim couple of days I remember. Then she got on to pornographic paper-backs and that finished it.

One night I came in very tired, and there she was standing up stark naked on the bed waiting for me, one breast painted green and the other one red. She looked so funny, I couldn't help it, I fell down laughing. I can still see her now, prancing angrily round the room with nothing on and her two-tone breasts—searching for this book, finding it, then standing in front of me pointing out the passage where it described a girl doing this and how the man who saw it went raging mad with desire. But all I could do was laugh. Poor Katie, she was livid that it didn't have the right effect.

Soon after that we finished, and Katie moved out. She went back to the Bayswater Road, and I settled down again to the peace and quiet of a different bird every night. I still think of her often now, whenever I pull up at traffic lights.

2

The Vertical Man

Was there ever anyone, at any time in your life, who was straight—
and of whom you thought it might have been possible, if you'd known
them better or spent more time with them, that they could have made a
difference to your way of life?

Yes, strangely enough, there was one, just one I knew once,
who I did think this of.

He was a teacher, used to come up once a week on a
Tuesday evening to one of the prisons I was in—eight, ten
years ago it must be now. He took an evening class in biology,
I think it was—at least, that was supposed to be his subject.
But to him there was no sharply defined limits, he used to
wander off into all sorts of other things—botany, geology,
archaeology, anthropology. He'd got many degrees and
honours in that field: but like all truly learned men he didn't
stick within the narrow confines of a subject.

He was getting on in life, must have been nearly eighty
when I knew him, and to look at him he was just like a novelist's
caricature of a scientist, almost too like it to be true. A great
halo of white hair, pink face, vague blue eyes that all the same
could suddenly become very penetrating and shrewd. Always
wore a crumpled old suit, his coat slung round his shoulders,
scarf flying about, tobacco-ash all over him. And a knobbly

walking-stick, which he really needed, it wasn't an affectation; there was never any pretence in him.

He came up to the prison all through one very bad winter, never missed once whatever the weather. Fog, snow, anything —he was always there, week after week. It astonished me that a man of his quality, his ability, should do it; especially as his class was only a small group of mugs all of my type. But somehow he gave the impression he did it not out of a sense of duty, not even out of enjoyment of parading his knowledge—which was enormous—but because somehow he felt this knowledge wasn't his to give or to hold back as he wished: he was only what you might call the custodian of it, and had to impart it to others whether they were worthy of it or not.

Some of the blokes, as you'd expect, used to poke fun at him, try to take the micky by asking the stupidest questions they could think of. But he never minded that. As far as he was concerned, even the stupidest thing had some matter in it, and since they'd asked he'd dig it out and give it in reply. His replies were so comprehensive, so vast in their sweep, that the bloke who'd thought to provoke him would end up knocked dizzy. Yet he was never taking a rise out of the man: he was humble and genuine and warm-hearted, with none of the cold-bloodedness usually associated with a scientist.

I used to sit and listen to him, absolutely fascinated by the brilliance of his mind and the quiet modesty with which he gave out his knowledge once he got going. After a time the weeks became all Tuesday nights, either looking forward to them or looking back and thinking about what he'd said. I got to the point where I started threatening the noisy ones in the class with a going-over if they didn't keep their stupid traps shut next time. Me—electing myself a sort of prefect, putting myself on the side of authority: it shows what an effect he was having that I'd do that for the first and only time in my life.

He was a little mad, a little eccentric, and that was why I

liked him also, because I've never been able to understand the entirely respectable and sane. But he was still shrewd enough to know the type of person I was. When I turned round on someone making a noise and said: 'O.K., you, shut up'—and they shut up—he knew it wasn't because I was respected or loved: he knew it was because the bloke was a bit afraid. And he knew what there must be in me in the way of viciousness to make the bloke feel like that.

So often enough, when he was answering some question I'd put to him, he'd gradually get the answer round to subjects like gentleness and humility, how being tough and self-important wasn't a very admirable quality, how fighting and bashing were no substitute for trying to use your brain.

He could get annoyed himself, but never with people— only about things, about subjects where he felt people were wrong in the way they looked at them. War, prejudice, starvation, intolerance—these were the things that made his eyes flash and his voice crackle. Yet I never saw him angry with any person: he gave the feeling that the quality he had above all was kindness towards other human beings. And it wasn't kindness to please himself, to give himself satisfaction at being kind. Myself, I can only be kind and never stop the self-congratulation that goes with it. But he had kindness—a different, natural, unthinking thing.

I never knew him condemn a point of view either, however much he opposed it. It was always a case of: 'I don't agree with what you say because . . .' Never: 'You're wrong and you shouldn't think that.' Whenever he gave advice, which was not when it was asked for but when it was needed, it didn't come out as instruction. Just: 'Perhaps if we could try to see it like this . . .' He knew what was right and what was wrong, and there were no two ways about it. He wouldn't shift, he wouldn't compromise on a principle, he wouldn't let you get away with any attitude he felt wasn't good. But always what he was doing was trying to make you think about it yourself, come round to the right conclusion yourself, not merely because he said so. He believed you would and you could, if only you learned enough about it. That was his job—to go on feeding you the knowledge, giving you the material on which you could work.

The whole fantastic, bloody thing about it was that I found myself believing he was right and trying to abide by his way of thinking—which of course couldn't possibly work, me being what I am. But somehow, for a period of months, while I was going regularly to his classes, some of his humanity and tolerance—a very little part of it—rubbed off on to me. In my whole life no one else has ever managed this, has ever even made me start to feel that their tolerance would befit me.

If I had the chance today, I'd work with that man for nothing. I've never met a man before or since who influenced me as he did, just very slightly towards the lines of civilization.

3

Talking late at night . . .

(We had been talking for hours, mostly about his childhood. Now the noises from the other furnished rooms in the house he lived in had all faded away. The quarrelling Irish upstairs had gone to bed, the Chinese girl had stopped shouting down the stairs to her friend, the German couple had finished playing their gramophone, the art student had come back from taking his bull-terrier its evening walk. Everything was silent and still, the only noise the occasional gurgle of the gravity-feed oil stove which heated the room. Bob was lying back in his chair, smoking, staring up at the ceiling. He was tired, and so was I. There were no more questions in my mind for that evening's session. . . .)

There's an old man I used to know . . . in his time this bloke had graduated up to the highest scales of crime, he was one of the best and most successful screwsmen in the business. But as he got older and kept on and on going back to prison, he sank further and further down, until eventually he was reduced to picking up suitcases on Liverpool Street station. I remember once being in a public house he used to go in a lot. Two of the police came into this place, went up to some blokes who knew him, and said: 'Look, that feller Joe, you're friends of his—for God's sake try and keep him off this thieving, will you, because if he goes into prison once more he'll never come out.'

I've seen a lot of these old men, you know, sixty or seventy years old, coming into prison with a sentence of ten years' preventive detention, and they won't ever come out. . . .

Do you see yourself ending up like that, trying to pinch suitcases on Liverpool Street station?

No.

Where do you think you'll be when you're sixty-five?

Dead.

And if you're not?

I'd better be . . . But on the eve of my life-time, do you mean, where shall I be then? . . . My common sense—which I get disgusted with, I hate my common sense—tells me I'll still be penniless and ignorant, just as ignorant as I am now, because of my indolence and all the other things I lack. Or maybe I shall be stinking it out in some prison somewhere, doing a fifteen stretch, wits dulled, mind full of bitterness . . . you can't expect me to follow common sense that far, that's why I hate my common sense when it starts leading to things like that. One doesn't dig very deeply into the future, you know, one tries just to live for the day and have no regrets. . . .

Do you have regrets?

Yes . . . just one. That I stole that two shillings from my mother.

Nothing else?

Nothing important. That I haven't ever given myself an education, perhaps. Yes, now I come to think of it, I do regret that quite a lot. There's one or two small things, trivial things, that I still want to do, like paint a painting or write a book—something that pleases me, that I've done myself, that has value to me, not to others. But I can't . . . because I'm not sufficiently educated. I'd like to be able to read things in French and German. Every time I read a translation I'm always conscious of the fact I'm missing something, the sort of flavour of the original. There are a few other subjects too I've always felt I'd like to know a bit about. Archaeology, anthropology . . . you remember when they discovered the coelacanth? I was fascinated by that, the whole thing fascinated me. I realized how little I knew, how dismally ignorant I was. I've often wanted to know more about things like that, there's so much one should know and could know. But I've always picked at things, never got down to them. . . .

Sometimes I feel if I'd had an education and knew something, however small, I might one time be able to pat myself on the back for something, tell myself 'Well done'. Yet I tell myself this sort of thing, but I know it's not really true. . . . Education needs hard work, concentration, determination—all the points I'm weakest on. The idea's just a pipe-dream, after all. To learn, to get an education even of an elementary sort, it'd take years—and like a child I see even one year as an impossible period of time. . . .

And then I think to myself—what for, anyway? Where could it get me, what does it matter? You see, I know it's too late, far, far too late, to change. I am what I am now; there's no going back.

So I content myself with the dream—the one that all criminals have—that one day I'll get the really big tickle. They've all got this dream: they're all going to get a big tickle and then they'll turn the game in for ever, set themselves up in a little business somewhere, retire.

That's all I can do now, take my time and wait for the chance to come. I've no intention of going straight, I'm just being more careful, that's all—and I'm getting cagey, I won't take unnecessary risks. It used to be I wanted a fifty-fifty chance, now I want it better than that, somewhere like seventy-five to twenty-five. But sooner or later it'll come, the job will be there, I'll do it, get the big tickle, and then I'll retire. . . . This is it, this is the dream, the great rock candy mountain that beckons us all.

And if I had it, if it came off . . . I still wouldn't open a business, I still wouldn't settle down and retire. I should squander it all like I've always done. I've had it before, I've had the chances and I've always done that . . . and I know I shall do it again . . .

Glossary of Underworld Terms Used in the Text

BIRD: 1 Term of imprisonment

    2 Girl

BOOT: Injure by kicking

BRASS: Prostitute

BUNG: Bribe

CANE: Iron bar

CASE, TO GO: To have sexual intercourse

CHARGE: Indian hemp

CHIV: Sharp-bladed weapon

CHOKEY: Punishment cells

CLOBBER: Pummel

CON: 1 Convicted prisoner

    2 Confidence trick

    3 Deceive with a confidence trick

COZZPOT: Policeman

DIP: Pickpocket

DRUMMING: Housebreaking

DUFFED-UP: Falsified

FIRM: Gang members

FLOWERY: Prison cell

GRASS: Informer

NICKED: 1 Caught

    2 Stolen

    3 Imprisoned

191

GLOSSARY

ONE-ER: £100

PETER: Safe

PONCE: Man who lives on a prostitutes earnings

POOF: Homosexual

PUSSY-HOISTING: Fur stealing

REEF: Fondle

SCHMOCKPOT: Useless

SCREW: 1 Prison officer

      2 Burgle

      3 Sexual intercourse

SPOUT, UP THE: Pregnant

STRIPE: Slash with a knife

TEARAWAY: Hooligan

TOM PEPPER: Liar

TOPPED: Executed

TURF: Prostitute's area of work

VILLAIN: Hardened criminal